D1609765

MERELY MELVILLE

BY THE SAME AUTHOR

Plays

CASTLE IN THE AIR
DEAR CHARLES
SIMON AND LAURA
JONATHAN
DEVIL MAY CARE
MRS. WILLIE
TOP SECRET
CHANGE OF TUNE
THE BARGAIN
(in America)
EVERYTHING HAPPENS ON A FRIDAY
TOP PRIORITY
GRANDE DAME
DEMANDEZ VICKY
(European production)
FEUNDER BITTE MELDEN
(European production)
CONTENT TO WHISPER

Fiction

WEEKEND AT THRACKLEY
THE VICAR IN HELL
11.27
DEATH OF ANTON
QUICK CURTAIN
THE CRITIC ON THE HEARTH

Non-fiction

MYSELF WHEN YOUNG
FIRST TIDE

Revues and Musicals

SWEET AND LOW
SWEETER AND LOWER
SWEETEST AND LOWEST
BETWEEN OURSELVES
A LA CARTE
SKY HIGH
AT THE LYRIC
GOING TO TOWN
ALL SQUARE
GAY'S THE WORD
(with Ivor Novello)
BET YOUR LIFE
MISS MARIGOLD
PRINNY
(in preparation)
CONGRESS DANCES
(in preparation)

T.V. Series

THE BRAINS TRUST
WHAT'S MY LINE?
MELVILLAINY
MERELY MELVILLE
MELVILLE MIXTURE
A TO Z
RAISE YOUR GLASSES
THE WHITEHALL WORRIER
THE VERY MERRY WIDOW
MISLEADING CASES
BEFORE THE FRINGE
LOOK AT LEACOCK
THE BRIGHTON BELLE
(in preparation)

MERELY MELVILLE

An Autobiography

by
ALAN MELVILLE

HODDER AND STOUGHTON
LONDON SYDNEY AUCKLAND TORONTO

ISBN 0 340 12594 2

PRINTED IN GREAT BRITAIN FOR HODDER AND STOUGHTON LIMITED, ST. PAUL'S HOUSE, WARWICK LANE, LONDON E.C.4, BY HAZELL WATSON AND VINEY LIMITED, AYLESBURY, BUCKS

To
J.K.

I

I WAS BORN—no, steady. That is no way to begin. Let us get down to the facts of life. I have died the death in, among many other places, the Opera House, Manchester; the Grand Theatre, Leeds; that place on the corner of Leicester Square where the three-course meal is the talk of the coach-trips and which used to be called the London Hippodrome; the King's Theatre, Southsea; and on innumerable occasions in the loony-bin. I mean the B.B.C. Television Centre, Wood Lane, London, W.12. Or as it is sometimes known, in deference to the B.B.C.'s past and present Director-Generals—and because of the bin's inaccessibility—the Greene Hill far away. The neatest act of necrosis at this last-mentioned address was a few years ago when Arthur Askey and I were doing a T.V. series called—I cannot think why—'Raise Your Glasses'. Except, I suppose, that we both wear specs. We were contracted for six shows, with the usual option on a further seven should we prove a riot and get in the charts. We weren't and didn't. We were, in fact, disaster. The millions who adore Arthur (myself included) bitterly resented me looming around in a dinner-jacket looking podgily po-faced; my three fans were furious when Arthur did one of his funny walks or said "ay thenk yew" a full two inches from the camera just when I was being tremendously witty. After the fifth successive script had been expertly cremated, there was a fairly sombre Court of Inquiry in the presence of a B.B.C. Top Executive: the kind of upper stratum with fitted wall-to-wall carpet in his office, a separate adjacent office for his secretary (sorry, P.A.), and a larger ashtray than the poor white trash on the third floor. I was the one who behaved. Everyone else screamed and yelled and hurled abuse and blame at each other; there was a moment when I thought the ashtray was going to join in the hurly-burly. I remained throughout calm, dignified, and—it goes without saying—po-faced. It is my natural expression; unless forced to smile or grimace professionally and for pay, I bear a marked resemblance to the Duke of Norfolk on an afternoon when he's been one of the stewards at, say, Lingfield, and not one of his own horses has even been placed. And then it happened. (It happens, too, on occasions with the Duke; usually after a tiff with Lord Wigg.) I felt a hot flush coming over me, the washerwoman in me came out like the puncturing of a pimple, and my first, last and only contribution to the discussion was to shout at the Top Executive, "The trouble with you, of course, is that you're a built-in shit!" The option was not taken up. On our way out of the Top Executive's office, Arthur said, "You know what he didn't really like, don't you? The word 'built-in'."

The necrophilic act in Leeds was on a Sunday night in 1948. If you write comedy, or try to, there is always one serious play inside you bursting to get out. The best thing is to get it out of the system as early as possible, and then forget about being a twentieth-century Ibsen or Tchekov. Thank God I did just that, but the labour pains in getting it out of the system were nothing compared to the post-natal complications. I had just written a sequence of revues—*Sweet and Low, Sweeter and Lower*, and *Sweetest and Lowest*—which had run for some five years at the Ambassadors Theatre. I know this is chickenfeed up against the nineteenth, or whatever it is, phantasmagorical year of *The Mousetrap*. But the Ambassadors is a tiny theatre, and in those days five years meant a lot. It certainly meant a lot to me. Although the book and lyrics of the first show—*Sweet and Low*—were mainly written by myself, there were other contributors, a fact which, naturally, I hotly resented. After all, it wasn't the first time I had had material of mine put on in the West End. It was the second. By devious means, some fair, some foul, I edged the others out, the two remaining revues were written entirely by me, and I was earning all of forty pounds a week. When the five-year stint began, I was an A.C.2 in the R.A.F., and forty pounds a week being paid into the bank in London seemed to me manna. By the end of the stint (again by devious means of the same assorted brands) I had become a Wingco, and I found that forty pounds a week meant even more. When you come home on leave as an A.C.2 in that rough and rather itchy pale blue ensemble with your forage cap at a provocative angle, no-one will allow you to pay for so much as a pale ale. Come back as a Wingco, in the peaked cap and the smooth made-to-measure number from Gieves, they expect you to stand vast rounds of double brandies. I suppose they think that as long as you are a humble A.C. plonk or an Army private or naval rating, you are having a quite terrible time and doing all the fighting; by the time you've reached the Wingco bracket or become a Lt.-Colonel or a Lt.-Commander, you're either permanently plastered in the Officers' Mess or having it off with some fraulein in München-Gladbach. In my case, it was quite the reverse. I had a ball as an A.C.2 (mainly in Skegness); the more promotion hit me, the nearer I got to the actual war. Which is, of course, a thing to be avoided.

So, too, is writing an allegedly serious play based on a biblical story with strong homosexual undertones and not a titter in it from start to finish. This was the thing I got out of the system immediately after the *Sweet and Low* revues. It was an attempt to dramatise the story of David and Bathsheba, and I don't think it helped much in 1948 to suggest that David was kinky for Jonathan. Perfectly true, of course, he was. His marriages were sad attempts to wipe out the past, or at least dim it: and they failed because they failed to do so. Nowadays such a suggestion wouldn't raise an eyelash in the upstairs room at the Royal Court even if you showed the pair of them stark naked and at it in each other's arms. Least of all, come to think of it, would a lash be raised in the upstairs room at the Royal Court. By the Royal Court I mean the theatre in Sloane Square, not David's Palace in Jerusalem. But in 1948 that sort of thing just Wasn't Done. We opened at the Aldwych on a stifling hot night in August; the congregation fanned themselves with their programmes from start to finish, which never helps. I think they and the critics were expecting another madly gay evening with parish-pump quips about Binkie and Ivor and Noël: they got a terrible shock. Mr. Harold Hobson, seen writhing in row C of the stalls, wrote: "The story of David and Bathsheba is told expertly in two verses in the second book of Samuel, chapter xi. Mr. Melville takes over two hours to tell it, and succeeds in turning it into a bore." Fair enough, I probably did. But I still consider it the best play I have ever written. I suppose most writers think that of their biggest flops. I saw it produced recently by the Amateur Dramatic Society in Lindfield in Sussex, and I must say the old thing stood up pretty well. I had a good cry in the last act and, to my intense satisfaction, I noticed that the Lindfield lady sitting next to me was also having handkerchief trouble. For one thing, it was better cast in Lindfield than in London. In London the part of David (who, to my way of thinking, was, apart from being homosexual, a poet, an aesthete, a dreamer and a schemer) was played by Mr. Leo Genn (who, to my way of thinking, is an absolutely superb portrayer of integrity and solid worth, but has few, if any, of these attributes or possible disadvantages). The part of the virgin Bathsheba was sustained, if that is the word, by Miss Coral Browne. And, although I love her dearly, if Miss Browne with not a stitch on had been about to take a bath on the rooftop of her house right opposite David's Palace, *she'd* have asked *him* over. Which would have ruined the plot.

But the initial dying of the death so far as *Jonathan* was concerned took place, as I said, in Leeds and not in London. Dress rehearsal: Sunday night. Only eight people in the theatre: Mr. Firth Shepherd, who presented the play; the director and designer; one of those publicity men who keep the whole thing an impenetrable secret; one or two hangers-on and myself. And for some extraordinary reason—I think he wanted to preach a sermon about it—a local vicar. There was a fabulous set by Anthony Holland, one entire wall of which took the form of a mural depicting a group of Assyrian warriors raring to go: spears poised ready to be thrown, and their legs (as Stephen Leacock once wrote) pointing to twenty-five minutes past seven. (Try it on your watch.) And the secret entrance to the Palace, through which Bathsheba —having been summoned to the King's presence—was to make her first appearance was between, through and under two of those legs. Miss Browne—the virgin Bathsheba—was wearing not a great deal of pure white butter-muslin, and had put her hair up and topped it with a small veil of tulle. There was a quiet religious hush in the theatre which impressed me. It was what I felt I needed and deserved after five years with Hermione Gingold. The hush was abruptly shattered when Miss Browne's veil caught in the apex of the Assyrian's triangle and she was yanked smartly back almost into the wings. In a voice which echoed round the West Riding (Miss Browne has a penetrating voice and quite a vocabulary), she said, "If anyone thinks I'm coming through this asterisk[1] crutch, they're asterisk well mistaken." Nor did she; after that she came down the stairs. We never found out whether the vicar preached his sermon.

[1] Asterisk was not the word used by Miss Browne. Mrs. Hodder wanted the actual word to appear in print; it was her friend Miss Stoughton who demurred.

II

An aunt of mine in Berwick-upon-Tweed, having unwisely patronised both *Jonathan* and a rather risqué revue
called *Sky High* starring, inter alia, both Miss Gingold and
Miss Baddeley, wrote: "... when I think that the last time
I saw you was at the Annual Dancing Display by the pupils
of Miss Knox's Preparatory School for the Sons and Daughters of Gentlefolk—you in your first kilt and sporran and the
patent leather pumps with the buckles your mother had
bought for you, and Miss Haliburton the dancing mistress telling me she was afraid you'd never get the hang of anything as
complicated as the Lancers—I must say, since you got in with
all this theatrical set, you've changed." I suppose I had.

No matter how you dodge it (as I have managed to do up
to now) sooner or later you must get down to, and gloss over
as quickly as possible, the Early Days routine. Berwick-upon-
Tweed is not a bad place to be born in; it is an attractive little
red-roofed or grey-slated town standing precisely on the
frontier between England and Scotland. In earlier skirmishes
between the Saxons and the Celts, the town changed hands
thirteen times, ending up English though situated north of
the Tweed. The last difference of opinion was in 1333, but
there is still a fair amount of doubt about status. The natives
(who are friendly even to newcomers to the town, given say
twenty years to get to know them) speak an odd mixture
of Lowland Scot and near-Geordie; the soccer team plays in
the Scottish League; your driving licence is renewed by the
Northumberland County Council; and the great thing is
that, being sensible, Berwick-upon-Tweed adopts English,
rather than Scottish, licensing laws in matters which have
nothing to do with driving a car—or ought to have nothing
to do with driving a car. This means that the pubs are open
on the Sabbath, and on or before the stroke of opening time
vast hordes of Celts are seen streaming across the border with
their tongues hanging out. It means a great deal to the town.

The geographical ambiguity of the town has also meant a great deal to me. When I have a play on tour and we play the Theatre Royal, Newcastle-on-Tyne, I am a dyed-in-the-wool, one-hundred-per-cent Northumbrian. I assume the Geordie accent (or try to) and can be heard saying things like, "Why, aye, man she's a canny buggor" over eleven o'clock coffee at Tilley's restaurant in Blackett Street. I have to explain that in Northumberland the word "bugger" is a term of endearment and is used more or less non-stop by well-dressed and dignified matrons over their coffee at Tilley's. Since my day, the restaurant has moved from Blackett Street, but I am sure the vocabulary remains; certainly many of the waitresses do. On Tuesday in the *Newcastle Daily Journal* the notice of my show is headlined "Northumbrian Playwright Flops Again". At the end of the week we move on to the King's, Edinburgh, where I become almost, but not quite, as Scottish as Andy Stewart. No-one, not even in Scotland, could be as Scottish as Andy Stewart. I hooch. I ask for champit tatties and neeps instead of pommes purées and navets à la crême. My accent switches from Edinburgh Morningside ("thet's a naice het") to Glasgow Gorbals ("och, awa' an' bile your heid") according to the company. On Tuesday in the *Edinburgh Evening News*, the headline of the notice is "Scottish Dramatist's Latest Disaster". Being a border-line case has great advantages.

The house in which I was born was, in fact, some four hundred yards south of the actual frontier. Not a sign of a plaque when I was last in the town, though there is one outside the King's Arms Hotel saying that Charles Dickens (1812–1870) Lectured Here. It was a large, unwieldy Victorian house called *Rowanlea*, rather wittily, we thought, because there was a long row of rowan trees lining the drive in the front garden. The house was in Castle Terrace, and everyone who lived in Castle Terrace was either rich or pretending to be rich; we were the ones who pretended most, and eventually had to give up the pretence. My father drank, and by the age of five I had decided that he beat my mother. This may have been dramatising, but he certainly never seemed very affable towards her. My mother was a much more than proficient pianist and painter, and gave the impression that she couldn't quite understand how she came to be mixed up in this sort of set-up. Which, I suppose, explains something—if not all—about me. It may be different now, but in those days—over fifty years ago—very few adults in Berwick painted or played the piano. If they did, they certainly didn't admit it in public. You did both at Miss Knox's Preparatory, but having left that admirable institution you put away such childish things. You fished; you played auction bridge or golf, but never the piano; and if you painted, it was either a new coat of white on the greenhouse or a slap of distemper where the walls had started peeling in the basement back-kitchen.

My father was a huge, florid man, permanently in knickerbockers, and with a fetish for punctuality. He was a partner in the family business (we were, and still are, timber merchants) and he cycled to and from work every day on a very tall, erect, black-enamelled bicycle which seemed to me to weigh a ton. He left on the dot of 8.15 each morning, taking down his bicycle clips from their allotted hook on the hall stand, and fixing them (for some reason I could never understand) round the nadir of his knickerbockers; he then cocked his leg over the saddle and pedalled off down the drive without a backward glance at my mother, who stood morning after morning at the top of the front door steps, waving. He returned on the dot of 12.45 p.m., slightly flushed (there was a steep hill and two pubs en route), poured himself out a stiff whisky and read the angling column in the *Scotsman*, and on the dot of 12.59 said, or more often than not shouted, "What's happened to *lunch*, for Christ's sake?" He put on his bicycle clips again on the dot of 1.15—lunch could be got through speedily, as there was no conversation : the old man had the *Scotsman* propped up in front of him throughout the meal—and returned at six, when he had three or four doubles while he sat at his bureau doing what he called his homework : vast piles of bills of lading and so on which he'd brought home from the timber yard to be checked. At 7.29 precisely he said, or again more often than not shouted, "What in God's name has happened to *supper*?," and having eaten it, he put on his clips again and cycled off to the Unionist Club to play billiards. He usually came back stoned. I used to lie in bed listening to him fighting losing battles with the hall stand trying to hang up his clips, and wondering how he'd managed to make the hill up to the house. I think the bike must have done it on its own, God knows it knew the way. I didn't really hate him. I don't think I really hate anyone, which makes me sound like Julie Andrews playing Rebecca of Sunnybrook Farm; but I certainly despised him. In 1923 he contracted double pneumonia and peritonitis and was going through what in those days was known as the Crisis. We had a day and a night nurse, and there was a great deal of drama in the house because the day nurse used the wrong saucepan for heating up water and the night nurse used the best china for making cups of tea at four in the morning and Maggie, the maid, objected. Just after the Crisis, the night nurse said to my mother, "I think he's on the mend; he's just told me to stop fiddling with his goddam pillows and get the living bejesus out of here." "Damn," I said. I was just under thirteen at the time. My mother said, "Alan, dear, *really*!" But she was smiling, and I don't think entirely because of the old man's potential recovery. In any case, he didn't recover. He had a relapse and died, and at the graveside ceremony a seagull plopped something unmentionable on top of the bowler hat with which I had been unexpectedly kitted out for the occasion. A rather hirsute distant relation standing next to me said, "Take a leaf, boy, take a leaf," adding for good measure, "it's a good job cows don't fly." My mother found that she had been left virtually penniless; Maggie had to go, and we had to take in a lodger. It caused the most frightful to-do in the Terrace; it was the talk of the Kenya Café, which was the Berwick-upon-Tweed equivalent of Tilley's for mid-morning coffee and hearsay. The lodger was an absolute cow, too, forever complaining about the bath-water not being hot enough.

I was four when World War I happened. In a broadcast a year or two ago, Sir Compton Mackenzie said he could remember things with absolute clarity from the age of four onwards, and so can I. Well, perhaps not completely "onwards". My trouble is that I cannot remember what I was doing last Tuesday, or the surname of someone I have to introduce whom I've been calling "Brenda, darling" for years, or where I put my dentures before tottering off to bed last night. If next morning they're not found down the side of the armchair in which I habitually sit, panic sets in. I once, having gone through the whole house with a fine tooth-comb (the obvious apparatus for locating lost dentures) rang my dentist and said, "I have a T.V. in three days' time, and I think I've thrown my teeth in the Esse. You've *got* to get me a duplicate in time." I then found I was wearing them. But, whereas the immediate past is fairly myopic, many of those early days of World War I are crystal clear. There was a night in 1915: we were living more or less permanently in the dining-room at *Rowanlea* to save coal, and my father had had his bureau brought in there and was doing his inevitable homework with the inevitable glass within easy reach. I had been sluiced and towelled down and was having my supper on the rug in front of the fire. The supper was a glass of milk and two boiled eggs beaten up in a mug (we had farmer friends), and the dressing-gown was bright red flannel with a navy blue cord with tassels. No kidding, I can see it all to this very day. My mother was knitting a Balaclava helmet (she had plunged herself desperately into war work even before the outbreak of hostilities was announced) and she suddenly said, "Alan—" (referring not to me but to my father). "I think I hear a zeppelin." My father paid no attention; he just took another swig of his Scotch and went on with his checking. It wasn't until the third or fourth time she said, "Alan, I'm *sure* I can hear a zeppelin," that he erupted. "Good God Almighty, woman," he said, "you've been hearing bloody zeppelins ever since this bloody war started. Come on out to the garden, show me. Bring the boy." We all went out and stood on the front door step and the zeppelin went directly over the house, flying very low and surprisingly quietly and looking like the underbelly of a whale. We made the boot-cupboard in three seconds flat. Father was there first. The zepp was brought down by anti-aircraft fire a few miles north of Berwick at a place called St. Abb's Head. Next morning mother and I went there and waded out at low tide, and mother cut off a little bit of the fabric with her nail scissors and pasted it in her wartime scrap-album, joining the adhesive portrait stamps of Kitchener and Haig and Marshal Foch. I still have it.

I have just remembered who Brenda was. Brenda de Banzie. I had to introduce her to two late arrivals at this cocktail party, and I said, "You do know Miss er-um-er-um . . ." She fixed me with a beady glint and said, "You've forgotten my name, haven't you?" "Darling," I said, "it is on the tip of my tongue." "If it is," said Miss de Banzie, "your tongue is more than usually furred."

I can, however, remember, just to show Sir Compton that he is not executing a *pas seul* in the Leslie Welsh business, the exact pattern of our hall linoleum. It was a very long hall, stretching from the front door to the dining-room at the rear of the house, and the lino was a rather pathetic attempt to give the impression of different-coloured wood inlays. Rather like the décor in the rapidly disintegrating

Pullman cars on the Brighton Belle. It was all in triangles, some dark bogus walnut, some pale phoney sycamore, various in-between shades which might have been imitation anything. The hall was polished daily by Maggie to such an extent as to make it lethal. Father had a great deal of trouble with it. The house had been cunningly planned by its Victorian architect (if it ever had an architect) so that the kitchen, which was in the basement, was as far away from the dining-room as possible. This meant that when my father gave his 12.59 muezzin call of "What's happened to *lunch*, for Christ's sake?" Maggie had to load the meal on to a black oval tin tray with little gilt squiggles round its edges (I can see that, too : Sir Compton must be livid), dart down a long damp passage in the basement, tear up the stairs (seventeen treads) to the ground floor, sprint along the lethal lino, and deliver the goods. One day it was mince, served on an out-size willow-pattern ashet with neat little segments of dry toast tastefully arranged round the perimeter. Maggie made the trip in just under eight seconds, but on reaching the dining-room door skidded on the lino and went arse-over-tip. Quite an extraordinary phenomenon happened; I have never witnessed such a thing before or since. The mince left the ashet not, as one would expect with mince, in individual particles but en masse, and described what I believe is known as a parabola. On one wall of the dining-room was a large lithograph of Queen Victoria in full gear. The mince landed with a dull plonk on the top of the lithograph's frame and dribbled very slowly down the imperial bombazined bosom, sashes and decorations. My father looked up from the *Scotsman*'s angling column, took off his pince-nez and said, "Maggie . . . we are not amused." It was the only time in my life I ever heard him say anything even remotely droll.

By this time, as I say, my mother had plunged herself into war work with a demoniacal frenzy. She dug up all her beloved roses and carnations and lily-of-the-valley and planted the whole of the back garden in potatoes, just in case. After all, the house was only a few hundred yards from a sea that until very recently had been known as the German Ocean, and you never knew. She was only restrained from digging up the tennis court in the front garden when the people next door said they fully intended to retain *their* tennis court and if the Germans landed, they would prefer to be shot playing tennis rather than whimpering in an underground shelter, eating raw potatoes. When the wounded began coming in, one of the local schools was commandeered as an emergency hospital with tents in the playground and mother was in like a flash, taking down Jeffrey Farnol novels and reading them out loud to the boys whether they wanted it or not. And, of course, knitting. At one time there were so many Balaclava helmets stacked high in the boot-cupboard, my father couldn't find his waders. I did my bit, too. Sphagnum moss was the thing to be collected in those days and, by God, I collected it. The trouble was that being even then as blind as a bat and not exactly botanically with it, I collected a good deal of other stuff. In the end the Matron of the hospital said to my mother, "We realise he's only trying to help, dear, but last week's collection consisted mainly of dried-up heather, lichen, and digitalis—which, as you know, is poisonous. *Could* you have a word with him? Perhaps he could confine his activities to flag-selling. Or *something*."

The fact that there was a war on didn't really, of course, affect us kids. We still foregathered in large groups, supervised by whichever parents were on duty roster that day, and armed with buckets and spades and bathing-costumes and towels and water-wings, set off for the beach at Scremerston, Scremmy. The Northumberland coast, south from Berwick-upon-Tweed to Alnmouth, consists of some twenty miles of the most glorious golden sands; if only it could be transferred to Brighton, where I now live, Cannes and Juan-les-Pins would be out of business. If only, come to that, it could be transferred to Cannes and Juan-les-Pins, instead of that miserable little strip you have to pay a fortune to lie on and show off, among other things, your French. Years ago I went down to the Ruban Bleu beach at Juan and said to the beach-boy in my very best French that I would like to rent a *matelot* for three weeks. I meant, of course, a *matelas*, one of those expensive mattresses that are obligatory on the Côte d'Azur in case you foul the *plage*. The *garçon* gave me a rather old-fashioned look, pointed to a corpulent character in maroon swim-trunks, and said in impeccable English that the gentle-man was a retired Admiral in the Free French Navy, but he didn't think he was that way inclined. In Brighton, even in mid-summer, I put on my swim-trunks, torture myself on the pebbles, and if the sea temperature isn't at least sixty I pretend I wasn't going in in any case, but was just looking for a friend; I then adjourn to the local or go and watch the dolphins. At least their pool is heated. Yet in those days we used to stay in the North Sea (or German Ocean) more or less all day, coming out of it only when summoned for a quick picnic lunch of banana sandwiches and hard-boiled eggs (which invariably got dropped in the sand but were still eaten) and then back into the deep-freeze. "Brave hearts and clean!" wrote (who else?) Alfred, Lord Tennyson. "And yet—God guide them—young!" We were young all right; I presume, having stayed so long in the water, we must have been clean; the thought of being brave never entered our heads. We simply stripped, went in and remained in until it was time to go home, when there was a fair amount of grizzl-ing and ill-feeling. I wouldn't go into the North Sea now for a thousand pounds. That's a lie, of course, I would. But for staying in longer than a couple of minutes the money would have to be upped.

Although, as I say, the war made very little difference to the juvenile population of the Terrace, every now and then we were brought up sharply and made to realise that it was on. One day the usual pilgrimage was on its way down the hill to catch the bus for Scremmy when a telegraph boy came toiling up towards us on his bright red bicycle. Even we knew that in those days a telegram usually meant only one thing. In charge of the posse that day was Mrs. Heriot, a gentle, very lovely woman who was a relation by marriage of my father's. We knew that her brother was fighting in something called the Somme, and though we hadn't been told very much about it, from the pictures in the *Illustrated London News*, the Somme didn't sound a bit nice. The whole gang of us stopped in our tracks and stayed stock still while the telegraph boy puffed and panted up the hill, dismounted, handed the telegram to Mrs. Heriot, and went off down the hill again, whistling. I can see the scene now. (I am beginning to feel quite sorry for Sir Compton.) Mrs. Heriot looked at the telegram for what seemed an eternity and then passed it to Mrs. McCreath, who was No. 2 on duty that day. There had to be two; one to keep an eye on the children while the other was getting the picnic and the thermoses ready. Mrs. McCreath opened the telegram with a slightly shaking hand, looked across at Mrs. Heriot, smiled, and said, "He's been awarded the M.C., dear." When we arrived at Scremmy we were all stood ice-cream cornets at the little beach hut.

Being a very excellent pianist, my mother was in constant demand throughout the war at all sorts of functions from sing-songs at the hospital to—on one occasion—playing in the orchestra pit of the local picture palace at a charity movie-show. This was not a success. For some reason, an outsize Labrador was in the audience and—no doubt entranced by mother's rendition of a medley of Sousa marches during the Pathé Newsreel—poked its head through the orchestra rail curtains and gave her a great, wet, slobbery lick up the right side of her face, being very thorough about it and taking it all in from chin to ear-lobe. My mother, who was obviously not expecting anything of this nature to happen, fainted

21

clean away in the middle of a Mack Sennett and musically the rest of the entertainment was as silent as the movie she was supposed to be accompanying. Another set-back, or at least change (uplift, you might call it) in her wartime musical career was when Dame Clara Butt and her husband, Mr. Kennerley Rumford, with the Band of H.M. Coldstream Guards gave a Grand Concert in the Corn Exchange. The price of admission went up as high as 7s. 6d., and for weeks before the event the Kenya Café was agog, mainly about what to wear. British Rail must in those days have been pretty much as it is today, because Dame Clara's piano was put on the train at Newcastle (where she had been ripping off 'Land of Hope and Glory' on the previous evening) and instead of coming to Berwick ended up in Carlisle. It was a Bechstein, and apparently it was unthinkable that Dame Clara could utter accompanied on anything other than a Bechstein. Ours was the only Bechstein in Berwick; it was yanked unceremoniously out of the house and further yanked up to concert pitch, from which naturally it never recovered. My mother's reactions to this were mixed. She was, of course, honoured to have saved the situation and thrilled that Dame Clara had actually leant on *our* Bechstein without buckling it. Later, when the flush of triumph had simmered down and she found she could no longer manage the top notes when accompanying herself in those trills at the end of 'The Pipes of Pan' from *The Arcadians* she used to mutter almost, but not quite, under her breath, "Bloody Clara Butt . . ."

It is hard to understand how anyone with this sort of background should resolve, quite early in life, to get into the theatre. Until I came along everyone in the clan had been so *respectable*. My father's side had been either timber merchants, sheep-farmers, or ironmongers and gunsmiths (my great-uncle dropped a cigarette-end in a stack of cartridges in the shop the family owned in the Berwick-upon-Tweed

High Street, blowing himself and the shop sky-high); my mother's lot were either sugar-refiners or in the ship-building industry. My mother was artistic, certainly; but artistry is not necessarily either hereditary or a *sine qua non* for muscling into show business. Until I was fourteen I had never been inside a theatre; the nearest were fifty miles or more away in Edinburgh and Newcastle, and after the death of my father the expense of such trips was out of the question. Anyway, my mother was too busy trying to get the bath-water hot enough for that dreary lodger. Theatre-wise, I was completely ignorant; I thought agate was a semi-precious stone. And if you live in a town like Berwick-upon-Tweed, you do not know of the existence—let alone read— such stimulating literary publications as *The Stage*, *Variety*, or *Plays and Players* (not that the last-named existed at the time). In any case, it had been made fairly clear that when I finished school (I had progressed from Miss Knox's to the local Grammar School) I would be going into the family business, and very lucky indeed to be doing so. Perhaps the first sign of impending doom was when we got a proper wireless set. Until then I had been scratching about on a crystal (oddly enough, the one station I could get at all clearly was Bournemouth, where a sister act seemed to be singing 'Bye, Bye, Blackbird' all the time); but the new set had a fretwork front, with green moiré silk showing behind the open bits of the fretwork, and three valves which stuck out of the top of the set. I used to print programmes in crayon, copying the details of cast and so on from the newspapers, sell these to my mother, force her to put the headphones on, listen intently and what is more applaud at both intervals and at the end of whatever the programme was. She was very patient about it all. One Christmas I was given (I think by Mrs. Heriot) a Pollock's Toy Theatre and this set me whirling off in all sorts of directions as author, director, choreographer, lighting expert, heaven knows what else. I tired very quickly of the characters and script supplied with the theatre (it was *Jack and the Beanstalk*, the plot of which goes distinctly ribby in the second half), but by cutting out photographs from magazines, gumming them on cardboard and sticking them on the end of those little wire prong things you had to shove through the slit at the back of the stage, some quite surprising dramatic works were presented. They were well ahead of their time, almost avant-garde. It was nothing out of the ordinary to find Queen Mary, Mr. Lloyd George, Mary Pickford, Mr. Hilton Phillipson (who was the local M.P.), the Archbishop of Canterbury and some rather unflattering drawings of my father all appearing together in a rollicking five-minute bedroom farce written by myself. My one regret is that I had grown out of the toy theatre phase by the time Mr. Phillipson, M.P. stopped being an M.P. because of some irregularity at a General Election, and his place in Parliament was taken by his wife who was an ex-Gaiety Girl called Mabel Russell. I could have written an even better part for her than for Queen Mary. I was mad about her; I spent hours shoving her election addresses into envelopes, and she never even noticed me. She was much too busy going round kissing everybody, which is why she won the by-election and, what's more, converted what had up to then been a Liberal stronghold (Viscount Grey of Falloden, Sir William Beveridge, and so on) into a comparatively safe Conservative seat. From which it has never quite recovered.

I also, of course, performed a good deal. In fact, considerable restraint had to be exercised to stop me performing. I had one absolute show-stopper in my repertoire : a recitation entitled 'Foolish Questions'. It was a fairly blistering send-up of our conversational inadequacies. It started off :

People ask such quite extraordinary questions
Which, if they paused to think, they wouldn't do.
I would like to make just one or two suggestions

24

On what to say, should this occur to you.
I told a friend of mine the other morning
That I'd just been to the funeral of Fred.
And he looked quite shocked and then said, with no warn-
    ing,
'But I'd no idea, poor fellow. Is he dead?' . . .

Foolish question ! . . . foolish question ! . . .
The reply should be "Oh, no, of course, he's *not*.
 He has been a little ill—
Just a cold : well, more a chill—
But we thought we'd shove him in the family plot.
Well, it's bound to happen sooner : maybe later :
So we thought we'd do it now : avoid the fuss.
And just think of what we'll save
Not to open up the grave.
But *dead*? Our *Fred*? Don't be rid-ick-u-luss !"

Come to think of it, it's the sort of thing George Robey
would have done splendidly. Perhaps he did. I gave it my
all; it never failed to bring the house down. I did it once in a
sailor suit at a concert in the Wallace Green Presbyterian
Church Hall in Berwick-upon-Tweed. The hall in those days
had a corrugated iron roof and I hadn't even got as far as the
first "Foolish question ! . . ." when the most almighty hail-
storm broke out and though I shouted—God knows I shouted
—not a word was audible. But I carried on to the end (there
were five verses and five choruses) and when it was all over
my elocution teacher said I was a little trouper. Infuriatingly,
the hail-storm stopped the instant I took my bow and exited
and the following item—which if I remember rightly was a
rather seedy lady greengrocer singing 'Pale Hands I Love'
from *The Indian Love Lyrics*—was listened to in a rapt
silence. That's show business.
    I suppose the real rot set in when my mother and I started

spending our post-holiday holidays in her own home town, Greenock. Greenock is on the Clyde; it has, or had in those days, a reputation for permanent rain, the smell of the sugar refineries, the clang (or worse, the silence) of the ship-building yards, and general depression and ugliness. After our annual holidays, it seemed to me Paradise. It was bustling and exciting; you could take cheap paddle-steamer trips down the Clyde and buy gooey Helensburgh Toffee in Helensburgh and—my God!—pay ninepence to watch the Rothesay Entertainers in Rothesay. Tommy Lorne, Dave Willis, Tommy Morgan, all the great Scots comics, outrageously, healthily vulgar, and experts at getting an audience in the hollow of the hands. For several years, our official annual holiday had consisted of going all the way from Berwick-upon-Tweed to Norham-on-Tweed (it was all of eight miles) where my father was a member of a syndicate which leased a stretch of the river for salmon-fishing. We stayed there for a month each year, living in a little anglers' inn called the Victoria. The drill was, to say the least, consistent. We rose very early every morning and had breakfast (trout), walked about a mile to the boat-house and then were rowed out by the boatman into mid-stream, where we remained until noon while my father cast and cast and cast and the boatman lapped and lapped and lapped very gently with his oars. If I rustled my comic, there was hell; if I said I wanted to be put ashore to spend a penny there was sheer bloody hell. At noon on the dot we were allowed back on the riverbank for a rushed picnic lunch (salmon sandwiches; father had his flask), then rowed back again to mid-stream and again marooned there until five, when we packed it in for the day, walked back to the Victoria for high tea (salmon) and went to bed. My father never seemed to have so much as a nibble until about the last three days of the holiday, when the beastly fish began leaping out of the water at him, demanding to be caught. We used to get back home with anything up to two dozen salmon weighing up to fifteen pounds or more; Maggie and mother had to boil them and then we gave all except one away. Usually to other anglers or the vicar. My mother, with her glasses steamed up over perhaps the ninth or tenth salmon simmering away in the fish-boiler on the gas stove, used to start muttering again. "Oh, God, what I'd give for a finnan haddock . . ."

It was in this mood, and still with a few salmon scales on her best navy blue costume, that we started going to Greenock. We stayed with my grandmother and grandfather, the latter being what is known as a card. He absolutely fascinated me. For one thing, he had a spittoon, placed not beside his own armchair by the sitting-room fireplace, but beside the chair opposite. This was to show off his prowess in saliva marksmanship, in the same way as some people boast about farting. He was the most terrible show-off. He spat into the spittoon at regular intervals—no more, perhaps, than once in every two minutes—and never once did I see him miss. I was thrilled. But the great thing was that there was a theatre in Greenock (in fact, there were three; now, naturally, there is none—at least no common-or-garden competitive commercial theatre) and my grandfather was a buddy of the manager, Mr. Wright, and had a complimentary box every Monday evening. On Monday after Monday we took a cab from Bentinck Street to the King's and it didn't take me more than three Mondays to realise that my grandfather was not genuinely theatrically-minded. I was installed by myself in the box and given either liquorice allsorts or a packet of assorted fruit gums, and grandfather said he had some important business to discuss with Mr. Wright and would collect me at the end of the show and if I wanted to go it was first on the left up the side of the dress circle. On the way home in the cab—his speech, I thought, just a little bit slurred—my grandfather would say, "Tell me what it was all about, boy. Your grandmother always likes to know."

And there, in the King's Theatre, Greenock, I saw magic . . . the Compton Comedy Company, *Katja the Dancer*, José Collins in *The Maid of the Mountains, Oh, Oh, Delphine!*, two girls I'd never heard of called Phyllis and Zena Dare who I decided would go far (I found out later they'd already gone far), the very early Scottish National Players being tremendously Scottish and National, the *lot*. And that, I suppose, settled it. There were even times when I got back to Bentinck Street with my liquorice allsorts unopened. My mother used to come to my bedroom and when I asked her what all the noise was in the living-room, she would say, "I think they're having a little argument, dear, nothing to worry about. Tell me : what was it like?"

We kept coming back to Greenock—to begin with for just a few weeks and then, when it was obvious that my mother was ill and unable to cope with the house in Berwick (and the lodger) for longer. By this time I was at Edinburgh Academy, and I spent my holidays in Greenock, not staying in my grandparents' house but with some good friends round the corner. I was getting on for seventeen; something was clearly wrong, and I wanted to know what. One morning I asked the doctor to tell me just what was the matter with my mother, I said I would rather know. He told me she had cancer and that it was incurable. I went back to the house I was staying in and prayed as I have never prayed before. I just prayed one thing, over and over again : let it be quick. I was walking round to the house in Bentinck Street early the next morning when I met the doctor again. He told me my mother had had a serious stroke late the previous evening; she died within hours. I know this may sound embarrassingly melodramatic—even square, which today is considered far worse : but I have always believed. I don't know at all clearly in what or whom. I have a feeling it isn't "whom", but in the absence at the moment of more precise information, God seems to me

28

as good a name as any to use. But I believe passionately that our lives are planned, however difficult it is at times to recognise the planning. And after that experience (there have been several more) why should one ever stop believing?

Oh, dear. There's a cast-iron case for the psychiatric couch if ever there was one. Hardly fair to take the money. Mother-fixation, fear, or at any rate, contempt of father. Wrong environment. Frustration in what one really wanted to do and saw no hope of ever doing. Fighting against one side of parental control, over-romanticising the other. Let's face it, she wasn't as good a pianist as all that, but to me she was Paderewski. I have counted : up to now I have used the word "mother" twenty-eight times. Oh, dear.

No wonder the boy grew up queer.

2

I THINK IT fair to say that I left Edinburgh Academy without making the slightest impression on it, either for good or ill. For a time I sat at a desk on which Cosmo Lang had carved his initials, which was supposed to be quite something to write home about; the desk I wanted to sit at was the one on which his brother Matheson had carved his. I won only one distinction of any kind during my brief stay—the Sir Walter Scott Prize for English Literature (Sir Walter was another Academical; you will gather that, between the two of us, the school has a considerable literary reputation); this was collected as a result of writing a parody on the works of A. A. Milne, who was all the rage at the time, if perhaps not with the members of the Academy 1st XV. "Collected" may not be the *mot juste*. The authorities had omitted to tip me off that I *had* won the prize, and at Speech Day I sat with the rest of the also-rans in the gallery of the school hall instead of among the prize-winners in the body of the hall. It was cosier up there; you could sleep through the speech by the Guest of Honour, Lieutenant-Colonel Sir Iain Mactaggart of Glenfiddoch, or whoever it was; or you could just go on eating caramels and flicking screwed-up caramel-paper on to the hats of the mothers below. When to my horror my name was called out and I calculated that it would take me at least five minutes to get out of the gallery to the exit, down the stairs at the back of the hall, all the way up the centre aisle and then up the few steps on to the platform, probably still with caramel on my face. I am all in favour of making a good entrance, but this seemed too long to keep them waiting. So I just stayed put. The Headmaster called my name three or four times, after which he raised his eyebrows in a forlorn Alastair Sim sort of way and the prize was put aside for later claiming. My mother was still alive at the time and had come from Greenock for the revels, still wearing her best navy. She was absolutely outraged by my non-appearance; it was one of the very few times I saw her really angry. "I have *never*," she told me subsequently in Crawford's Tea-Rooms in Princes Street, "been so affronted. And don't just sit there, stuffing yourself with Bath buns. Say you're sorry." I had to collect the prize next morning from the Headmaster's study; it was the complete works of Sir Walter and I dropped the lot on the way out. The Headmaster said, "Dear God! ..." and did another Alastair Sim with his eyebrows. He even did the mournful sagging jowl business while I was picking the books up.

There was much that I enjoyed about the Academy, and a good deal that I wasn't so keen on. My sporting activities were, and are, confined to swimming, tennis, roulette and the horses, none of which the Academy dealt with in my time (it has since acknowledged tennis, and with success); cricket has always seemed to me a game not to be played but to be watched half-asleep in a deck-chair or, better still, as I do it nowadays from the pavilion of the Sussex County Ground in Hove, following the play through the bottom of a glass, darkly. In any case, it had not then been found out just how short-sighted I was, and I could never see the ball until it was within a yard or two of me, by which time it was too late. I was equally hopeless at rugby; I think I once got as high as a place in the 6th XV, but usually it was the 7th, and once I was demoted to the 8th, which was very embarrassing as I was at least three years older than anyone else in the side. My one triumph at rugby was not at school, but at Berwick after leaving school. The local team must have been absolutely stuck and scraping the bottom of the barrel, because I was given a place in the side and to my horror quite early in the game the ball came out to me on the wing. What is more I caught it and managed to hang on to it. I was tackled just below the midriff by some sadist from Melrose, but I have a lot of midriff and managed to wriggle free. This was around our own twenty-five and the chances of getting anywhere near the opposition twenty-five, let alone scoring a try, seemed minimal. But I set out. The spectators were shouting, "Alan!" ... "*Alan*, for God's sake! ..." but naturally I took these as shouts of encouragement. The opposition seemed strangely lethargic about making any attempts to stop me in my tracks; they appeared almost hypnotised and one or two of them were doubled up as though in pain. I scored the try all right, dead between the posts, and then discovered that in the tackle the gentleman from Melrose had removed most if not all of my pants and I was revealing the lot.

Edinburgh Academy is approximately two-thirds a day school and one-third boarders. For the boarders, such as my-self, life was fairly Spartan. I was due to begin my first term on the day my father died, so I was some days late in appearing on the scene, being taken up to Edinburgh by some aunt or other and dumped. The rest of the new boys had started to settle in and I was greeted with a mixture of curiosity and sympathy; the thing that really irked me was that all the beds round the walls in the dormitory had been taken up and I was left with the one in the middle. Reveille was at 6.45 and we had icy cold baths in copper tubs, followed (after, of course, putting on some clothes) by porridge so thick that you could stand your spoon upright in it and it didn't give a millimetre either to port or starboard. There was a boy in the dormitory who was highly averse to early rising; his bed was at the opposite end of the room to the door leading to the tubs, so that when he eventually got up he had to run the gauntlet. This was made more interesting for him by the fact that the rest of us throughout the gauntlet-running flicked him with the ends of our towels—which, if wet, which they invariably were, and with a small knot tied in the wettest corner, made quite serviceable flickers. As he almost always had an erection on getting up, the flicking possibilities were even more exciting than just catching him on the bare arse. There was another boy—I forget his name, which will cheer up Sir Compton—who was a Roman Catholic and who knelt beside his bed every night and said very lengthy prayers. We respected him for doing it, but it embarrassed us enormously; the moment he got off his knees and in between the sheets there was a sigh of relief and we started off again telling what we imagined were dirty stories.

The head of the dorm was a boy called Ronnie, who was also head of the House, captain of the cricket XI, and just about everything else. I was absolutely mad about him. He was several years older than me, and really we had nothing in common; he was extremely good-looking and brilliant at games, and even in those days I was podgy and a duffer. I think the only thing we shared was the same brand of sense of humour; when he laughed at something I said, I felt I was on that Mittel-European state I appeared in not long ago with Cilla Black : Euphoria. After prep throughout the summer term we had fielding practice on one of the cricket pitches behind the Houses; he used to hit up half-a-dozen cricket balls in quick succession, giving them the most almighty swipes high in the air for the rest of us to catch; you were only allowed back in the House when you'd caught three running. It goes without saying that I was always the last to be returned to base; dusk would be falling while balls were still slipping with ease through my butterfingers and the dusk, combined with my short-sightedness, of course made the whole thing more difficult. "Look," he said one night. "Will you *try*? Just *try*, for my sake." "Yes, Ronnie,"

I said. "I'll try. Honestly, I'll try." I cannot think what came over me—some miracle, I imagine, comparable to the dividing of the Red Sea—but in half-an-hour I never dropped a single catch. When he said, "Okay, fine. Let's pack it in," I even said, "No, just another five minutes," and went on making one spectacular catch after another, frequently showing off and using one hand only when two would have been more orthodox and safer. Trying, concentrating for once, I suppose, for Ronnie's sake. When we did eventually pack it in and walked back together to the House, he said, "Well done, Mellers." I was waiting for him to put his hand on my shoulder and give me a little manly pat in a Rudyard Kipling sort of way, but he didn't. But before the lights were put out in the dorm that night we winked at each other from our respective beds. This beautiful friendship (which, I have to admit, never got even as far as a little innocuous feely-feely behind the fives court) had its occasional setbacks. There is an institution at Edinburgh Academy called the clachan. It is really an item of sporting equipment, consisting of a flat oval-shaped piece of hardwood on the end of a long stick, but it can be used for non-sportive purposes—mainly discipline, which at the Academy, unless the crime was a really serious one, was dealt out by the senior boys on the behinds of the juniors. Friday night was torture night; we had to learn by heart the names of those selected to play in the 1st XV on the following day; we were summoned into the senior boys' common-room one at a time and had to reel off the team in its correct order and at speed. I was hopeless at it, which must be of some consolation to Sir Compton. After several successive weeks of getting as far as the scrum-half and then drying completely, I was told that Ronnie wanted to see me in his study. He was brewing hot chocolate (the head of the House had all sorts of privileges like that) and he looked genuinely concerned. For a moment I thought he was going to offer me a mug of chocolate, but he didn't. "What's the matter?" he said. "You just don't seem to *care*. Is there something worry-ing you? Is there anything you'd like to tell me?" There was, of course, but I didn't feel it was the right time to come out with it. I mumbled something about being sorry and I'd try to do better next week, and he suddenly said, "Right: bend over" and gave me six absolute belters with his clachan. "The trouble with you," he said, "is that you're *wet*." I went straight to the bogs and cried my eyes out. Not at the effect of the clachan, though my backside was still stinging, but at being called wet. By him, of all people. I met him a few years ago in London. Still very handsome, but an old man, ill, and with snowy-white hair. It gave me quite a shock. The next time I had what remains of my own hair cut I looked down as the clippings fell on the sheet festooned round my neck and shoulders. Most of them were the same Nordic blond my hair has always been. Well, some of the clippings were what you might call ash-blond. Well, ash. Well, let's face it, white.

As if Ronnie was not enough to disturb someone who had had no sex education (the nearest I got to that was my mother saying, in putting me to bed, "Now *do* try to be a good boy tonight"), we had mackintosh trouble. There was a long hall in Jeffrey House, where I was boarding, where all our coats, scarves, school caps, and so on were hung up; and one of the new boys who had enlisted in the same term as myself had been kitted out with a shiny black rubber mackintosh. It fascinated me; I used to feel it surreptitiously when passing along the corridor and once, greatly daring, I sneaked it off its hook and tried it on in the loo. It had a quite remarkable effect. I knew nothing, naturally, about fetishism in those days; it just gave me enjoyment. Later I began to get very worried indeed about it; I imagined I was the one and only person in the whole world to have a thing about this sort of thing, and that it was something to be ashamed of and ought to be fought against. Later still, when I found it was a fairly

35

common kink, I was vastly relieved. I gather that it usually goes with various forms of sado-masochism, which is something I have never gone in for. I have a feeling it might hurt. But I got a kick out of wearing the kind of mack I tried on in the bogs of Jeffrey House over forty-five years ago, and I still do. Crazy.

I learned later that, when my father died, there had been some sort of family conclave and various relations had agreed that—having been entered for the Academy—I should go there as planned and they would guarantee the fees and other expenses, and then consider the possibility of my going on to Edinburgh University. For which I have always been and still am very grateful. I think there must have been another conclave, because when I was seventeen it was decided (no doubt after reading my end-of-term reports) that further education would be a dead loss and that I should leave school as quickly as possible and go into the family business. This was now run by my father's cousin, Uncle James (husband of the lovely Mrs. Heriot), who was a brisk military type with all the wrong ideas about starting at the bottom and working one's way up. I served my five years' apprenticeship as a joiner, beginning at 7s. 6d. a week and spending the whole of my first year doing nothing but boiling the glue and sweeping up shavings. In the second year, when my stipend was upped to 10s. od. a week, I was allowed to do a little planing of the planks of deal used to make door jambs (the firm had a quite flourishing business in manufactured joinery, and has a much bigger one nowadays); in the third year (12s. 6d. a week) I was entrusted with a chisel and can still show you the scar on my right hand where the chisel slipped and fourteen stitches had to be inserted. And so on for, as far as I was concerned, five completely wasted years in which I was of no use whatever to the firm and the firm was of no benefit to me ... except that I suppose, if pressed, I could still make a door or a window. It probably wouldn't open or shut, but at least I could go through the motions of assembling it.

I went through the daily chores at the timber yard numbly and automatically, all the time thinking about the impossibility of ever escaping. Young people are more free now to decide their own future; it is no longer taken for granted, thank God, that because your father was a timber merchant or a plumber or a criminal, the son and heir must necessarily want to follow in father's footsteps. The one and only incident that sticks out in my mind during those long bleak years was when one of the machinists in the joiners' shop omitted to put the guard on his machine and all five of the fingers on one of his hands flew almost the entire length of the shop. He had the presence of mind to switch off the machine before passing out, which was certainly shutting the stable door after the horse had bolted. None of us would pick up the fingers. In the end they were swept up with the shavings and sawdust which permanently littered the shop floor, and put in the boiler.

During part of this time I stayed with my paternal grandmother and her two daughters (who were even then in their fifties) in a huge and hideous stone-built house of which they only seemed to occupy one room which was known as the library; I think because it had bound volumes of *Punch* in it, from the very first issue. My grandmother was an extremely hairy old lady; she had quite a beard. She also had a very ancient Scottish terrier who smelt to high heaven and had a permanently filthy behind which, to its credit, it used to try to clean by dragging it along the hall carpet. The two daughters were complete opposites; one, who had married a parson who died on her almost as soon as they came down the aisle, was soft-spoken and gentle; the other, who was unmarried, seemed to me bitter, hard as nails, and an absolute bitch. Oddly enough, years later when I really got to know her, I found her great fun if slightly exhausting. She stayed with me for a month every summer and by the end of the month I was worn out. She was slightly peeved when I moved from London to Brighton, which she found too quiet (she was well over seventy by this time), but we went up to London each day and her idea of a day's relaxation was to take in the National Gallery or the Tate and either Fortnum's or Harrods in the morning, then have lunch (she preferred Rules), then a matinée followed by tea (Derry and Toms' roof-garden if fine, the Ritz if wet), then a little brisk window-shopping or perhaps a news cinema before an early dinner (back to Rules; she was a great favourite with all the waiters there) and then a show in the evening and bacon and eggs and a glass of sherry on the 11 p.m. Brighton Belle. She was quite genuinely cross on the final Saturday of her last visit when she found that, in addition to doing the matinée, she could have taken in two shows in the evening, one at 5.30 p.m. and a different one at 8.30, and still managed a quick snack at Rules in between. She usually organised her visits to coincide with Wimbledon; like myself, she was a mad tennis enthusiast. On her last visit, I had fixed up centre court seats for the pair of us on one or two days each week; on one afternoon it was blazingly hot and she had a slight but unmistakable heart attack. I was engrossed in a somewhat tense encounter in which it seemed possible that for once Rod Laver might be beaten (he wasn't, naturally) and didn't even notice. How long she remained slumped at my side I have no idea; eventually she was carted off by one of those hefty and highly efficient stewards from the Services they have at Wimbledon. He picked her up as though she was a feather, which she wasn't, and whisked her over the heads of the spectators and out with the minimum of fuss. It was the start of the finish; a few weeks later she was found dead all by herself in the basement kitchen of that damp dreary house in Berwick, with a single cracked cup and saucer on the kitchen table and a battered old saucepan on the gas ring and the gas jet still lit. In the enormous kitchen cabinet only a few yards away from her were four complete dinner services of the most gorgeous china—Doulton, Worcester, the lot; twenty-four of everything. Twenty-four soup plates, twenty-four dinner plates, twenty-four dessert plates, twenty-four side plates; all the tureens and sauceboats and other trimmings. I suppose, apart from being taken out and dusted at the annual spring cleaning, not a single plate had been used for thirty years.

That was typical of the way the trio lived. The Ladies' Bridge Club came to the house on the last Tuesday of every month; on the morning of the great day the drawing-room was opened up, the dust-sheets taken off the chairs and settee, the room swept and aired, and the best silver brought out of the drawers where it had been stowed away carefully wrapped in tissue paper. When the bridge session was over, the dust-sheets were put on again, the silver re-wrapped and put away, the drawing-room door locked for another month, and the trio went back to living in the library or Black Hole of Calcutta with the ponging Scottie. They were kind, but we really didn't get on; one of the two sisters would always be sitting up with a martyred expression when I came in late from tennis, sometimes as late as ten o'clock. They did their best not to show it, but I am sure they were genuinely relieved when I announced that I would like to be on my own and was going to take a room in the Waterloo Hotel. By now I was a junior costing-clerk in the timber business, earning three pounds a week less a number of small deductions which I didn't quite understand but resented. The Waterloo was run by an energetic saint called Miss Nellie Robertson; she let me have a microscopic back room for thirty shillings a week, for which I got a colossal breakfast, an excellent three-course lunch, a mountainous high tea, and was free to raid the kitchen or the larder later in the evening if feeling peckish. Most of the inmates were commercial travellers; there was one other permanent resident, an outsize lady called Miss Buchanan who was slightly potty and wore enormous hats, liberally plastered with large cabbage roses. She made a point of changing before sitting down to her sausage and egg high tea. The Buchanans, she kept telling everyone, always changed for the evening meal. They were, of course, the Glasgow Buchanans. The sweet people. Her father had died a millionaire. Miss Robertson had great difficulty in getting her to pay her bill.

I was a member of the tennis club, the badminton club, the hockey club, the Berwick-upon-Tweed Amateur Dramatic Society, the Berwick-upon-Tweed Amateur Operatic Society, and Heaven knows what else. It was all go. But all the time was the nagging problem : how in God's name could I ever get away? The answer—or at least the first pointer to the escape route—came through, of all things, the late-lamented *John o' London's Weekly*. In 1932 this admirable journal ran an essay competition—two hundred and fifty words on 'My Perfect Holiday' : first prize a return trip to Canada on the *Empress of Britain*. I won. The morning I heard the news I went over to the timber yard (it was on the south side of the river, and though I was on my bike I have the distinct feeling that I floated across) and broke the news to my uncle. "You're not going, are you?" he asked. "Well, of course," I said. It occurred to me later that I really ought to have asked his permission to take the fortnight off, but for once he was rendered so near-speechless at the idea of my winning anything that he just said, "Good God!" and went back to his private office. Anyway, he docked two weeks from my salary.

The *Empress of Britain* was a lovely, gracious ship; when she went down in the Second World War, I gave a long, sad "aaaahh! . . ." on hearing the news on the radio. It was all slightly overpowering for a twenty-two year old who until then had never even been to London; I had the first of several hot flushes when the cabin steward insisted on unpacking my one rather tatty suitcase and said he would lay out my pyjamas. I hadn't any. The passenger list (I still have a copy) more or less tells its own story :

Mrs. W. H. Hartshough, jnr.
Mr. E. H. Hinkle.
Mrs. Hinkle.
Master J. E. Hinkle.
Miss Gertrude M. Howard, M.A.
Mr. E. Hollingdale.
Mrs. Hollingdale.
Miss N. Hollingdale.
Miss P. Hollingdale.
Miss R. Hollingdale.
Count Antoine de Hubert.
Mrs. Frank B. Hughes.
Mr. Edgar J. Hughes.
Mrs. F. Hunt.

Looking back, I have the feeling they were all cracking bores; in fact, I think I came to that conclusion at the time. However, after the initial pyjama embarrassment, I got on splendidly with the stewards. I liked Montreal as much as anyone can like a city on a visit lasting one day and a night; and I adored Quebec. Steep narrow winding streets with buggy-carts clopping up and down them; old cannons facing out over the St. Lawrence through openings in the ramparts just as they do over the Tweed at Berwick; exciting words like "blanchisserie" and "alimentation" on the shop-fronts; the Chateau Frontenac, where I stayed, towering over the city and the Heights of Abraham towering over the Chateau Frontenac and putting even that magnificent hotel firmly in its place.

The return trip on the *Empress* was much gayer. Both the Olympic Games and the Commonwealth Conference had just ended in Ottawa; the passenger list this time was neatly divided between Lord Burleigh and several hundred hearty young athletes in navy blue blazers who tore round the promenade deck at all hours of the day and night, and Mr. and Mrs. Stanley Baldwin, Neville Chamberlain, J. H. Thomas and family, Sir John Gilmour, someone called Sir Atul Chatterjee who seemed to appear for each meal with a different posse of ever lovelier Indian ladies in ever more gorgeous saris, and a great many more. Mr. and Mrs Baldwin went for slow, solemn walks round the promenade deck, gravely dodging the athletes as they pelted past, and dressed as though about to attend divine service in Nuneaton. Mr. Thomas danced everyone else under the table, and on occasions more or less ended up there himself. Mr. Chamberlain remained in his cabin throughout, no doubt trying to work out what to tell the Press on getting back to Southampton. From what one gathered, the Conference had achieved precisely nothing and this always calls for delicate phrasing.

The great thing about this trip was that it made me realise that, as it seemed unlikely that I would ever go direct from a back room in the Waterloo Hotel, Berwick-upon-Tweed, to stardom in the West End, there was a possible side-entrance through writing. It had taken me about half-an-hour to write the *John o' London* essay; the thing was obviously money for old rope. I bought a very rickety second-hand typewriter and as soon as I got back from the timber yard and put down my high tea, I started bashing away at it in my little cell. The commercial travellers in the rooms on either side of my own used to thump on the walls at one in the morning, and every now and then would shout out, "For Christ's sake, *shut up* !" but I carried on regardless, kidding myself that I was typing pianissimo. I worked it out that, if I was going to end up in show business, the only hope for a junior costing-clerk in a place like Berwick was to get in on sound radio. Then I would meet the Right People; Val Parnell would get to hear about me, recognise in a flash that I was completely wasted in the sticks, and would whisk me to London to write, if not necessarily to star in, the next show at the London Palladium. Again the geographical dubiety of Berwick-upon-Tweed came in handy; I could decide whether graciously to offer my talent in the first place to either the B.B.C., North Region, or the B.B.C., Scotland. After the toss of a coin, the decision went in favour of the North, I wrote six short stories for the North Region Children's Hour called 'The Adventures of the Pink Knight.' They were quite unbelievably awful; a mixture of smug and twee; but they were accepted—at two guineas a script. I cannot believe how I had the nerve, but I wrote back and said I would only permit my material to be performed if I broadcast the stories myself. The B.B.C., reeling back understandably, said that I would have to have a voice test, adding that—in the unlikely event of passing the voice test—the fee would remain the same: two guineas all in, and no expenses. I passed the voice test, and in 1934 had my first professional engagement. Again looking back, I feel quite sorry for Uncle James at the timber yard; which was no easy thing to do at the time. I just said, "Oh, by the way, I'm broadcasting from Manchester on Wednesday; won't be in." The return fare from Berwick to Manchester in those days was around 28s. 6d.; by eating as little as possible and pretending to have a taxi laid on from the Manchester studios to the station (and then running to the station through the rain) it was possible to get back to Berwick only a few shillings in the red. But it was worth it. They liked the stories and, for some extraordinary reason, they liked me. A nice, cosy woman who played the piano in the North Region's Children's Hour programme said, "You must come back, luv." Her name was Violet Carson, now better known as Ena Sharples in 'Coronation Street.'

By now the writing bug had got me. It is an insidious little creature; once it gets inside you, no amount of insecticide (or even rejection slips) will get rid of it. Pope asked:

Why did I write? What sin to me unknown
Dipped me in ink—my parents', or my own?

In my case, the answer was perfectly straightforward. I wrote
for money, and still do. But in the mid-thirties I wrote in
order to save enough money to get out of Berwick and free
of the trap I imagined I had found myself in. It was an un-
grateful attitude, considering how generous and kind so many
people had been to me; but it was the truth. I wrote anything
and everything and most of it came straight back in the
stamped, addressed envelopes I enclosed with the manu-
scripts. But there were occasional acceptances : maudlin sentimental poems for the *People's Journal*, more short stories for
Children's Hour, brief paragraphs for the now deceased Glasgow *Bulletin* called 'Little Bulletins.' These were paid for at
the rate of five shillings a paragraph and it did occur to me
that at this rate of payment it was going to be quite some time
before the escape could take place; but sometimes I was able
to sell three paragraphs a week, and I just kept on churning
the stuff out. Tucked under the pink and yellow costing-cards
on my desk at the timber yard were sheets of paper on which
I was scribbling things that had nothing to do with doors or
windows or mortices and tenons; at night in the little room
in the Waterloo Hotel the typewriter keys were red-hot and
the adjacent commercial travellers thumping on their walls
more angrily than ever. I wrote a novel—a whodunit called
Weekend at Thrackley; it wasn't very good (in all the six
whodunits I have written I have committed the most sensational crimes in the first chapter without properly working
out how they were to be solved in the last, and this shows),
but to my amazement it was accepted first time out by a sub-
sidiary of Hutchinsons, sold rather well, went into paper-
back, and was subsequently made into a film called, for no
reason that I could fathom, *Hot Ice*. The film was quite terrible and bore no relation at all to the original masterpiece. I

then took stock of the situation. I had earned much more through the three months it had taken me to write the whodunit in my spare time than I could have earned in three years at my present emolument in the timber business. I rehearsed my lines for several days in my room at the Waterloo (in the unaccustomed stillness the commercial travellers must have thought I had died) and I then went, rather red in the face, to my uncle and asked if I could have a rise on my three pounds a week. My uncle, also going rather red in the face, said no. "In that case, Uncle James," I said, going puce in the face, "I give you a month's notice." There had not been a bigger sensation in Berwick-upon-Tweed since Berwick Rangers played Glasgow Rangers in the first round of the Scottish Cup and the Glasgow Rangers supporters went through the town systematically flinging empty beer and whisky bottles through all the shop windows that weren't boarded up and peeing on the War Memorial. The Kenya Café was even more agog than it had been over Dame Clara Butt or my mother's lodger. After all, I would, I suppose, in due course have become a director—perhaps even the managing director—of the firm; thank God I didn't. I would have been hopeless at it, and today it is in the more than capable hands of Uncle James's son, who has all the right ideas about running the business and is, as a likable bonus, a charmer and fun. Sometimes I think heredity is wildly overexaggerated. Uncle James, after I had delivered the ultimatum, went straight to my dearest friends in the town, Dr. and Mrs. Mclagan, and told them what had happened. Being my dearest friends, they at once reported his reactions to me. His first reaction was to ask for a large Scotch. His second was to come out with a not very Christian but, I suppose, understandable observation. "I hope he suffers," said Uncle James. "By God, I hope he *suffers*."

For the next few years I free-lanced and there were many

45

occasions when I felt that Uncle James's hope was being fulfilled. With the money from the film rights and by raising a mortgage, I bought a small plot of land in Tweedmouth not far from the family business I had left to struggle along without me, and had a mini-bungalow built on it. One sit., two beds, kit., and bath. I called it *Thrackley* after the whodunit; it had red brick walls and a green tile roof which made it look rather like a garden gnome. It was by no means handsome to look at, but it was the first place I could really call my own. The garden, both back and front, had been part of a field which obviously hadn't known the swoosh of a plough in decades and was filled to overflowing with enormous boulders. After several years of hard labour on it, I had just got it right, or almost right (no garden is ever *right*) when I had to sell up and leave. I had also invested in a fairly lethal motor-cycle; when we knocked off playing tennis every evening in the summer, or badminton or attending the Operatic Society rehearsals in the winter, a gang of us—all fore-runners of the mods and rockers—used to tear across the Royal Border Bridge and up the hill to the bungalow, where we played pontoon and drank a great deal of beer. It was the first time in my life that I felt I could do as I liked. The only persistent trouble was finance. The subsequent whodunits didn't make nearly as much as *Weekend at Thrackley*; not a glimmer of a film sale from any of them. I wrote one supposedly humorous novel under another name, thinking that perhaps first novels sold better than second or third ones; this one sold several thousand fewer copies than any other book I'd written, so I went smartly back to being Alan Melville. I kept a meticulous note of my earnings and some months they were in single figures, not double. One month they were in shillings, not pounds. One day when I went nervously into the National Bank of Scotland in Bridge Street, the cashier pushed my statement across the counter to me, and it was all too clear that the final figure was in red. I was furious because he positioned the statement so that the lady standing beside me waiting to be served (who was one of the biggest gossips in the town, which was saying something) could have no difficulty in assessing my financial status. She put on her reading glasses at once, I noticed, trying to give the impression that she was about to write out a cheque. I sent a fairly stiff letter to the Bank Manager, pointing out quite irrelevantly that his son was at Edinburgh Academy and was in fact wearing some of my cast-off school gear, and saying that I had always assumed that one's bank balance was a private matter between the Bank and the clientèle, and not something to be flaunted like a poster in front of all and sundry. It kept them quiet for a few weeks. I had one dread : that I would be forced to crawl back to the timber business, say to my uncle that I was very sorry, and ask to be taken back.

The B.B.C., bless them, saved the situation. I had been writing quite a lot of revue material for them, mainly for their station in Aberdeen, which was run by a very bright spark called Moultrie Kelsall, now well-known as an excellent character actor in the Scottish theatre and on T.V. I was also still playing the dual-nationality role, plying the B.B.C. in Manchester with sketches and lyrics and other scripts as a staunch North Countryman. I had had the good fortune to find a tame composer; his name was George McNeill; he was a commercial traveller for some seed firm in Edinburgh and he came to Berwick once a fortnight, and we got round the old second-hand upright piano in the bungalow (the Bechstein had, of course, been sold and in any case wouldn't have fitted) and together we turned out number after number. He was a good pianist, a more than good singer, and the lyricist's idea of the perfect composer. In other words, I lah-lah-lah'd the tune to him and he wrote it down. He was queer, and some years later was murdered by a regrettable young man he invited back to his flat in Glasgow. As a partnership, we reached the stage when Mr. Kelsall in Aberdeen, the Head of Variety in Edinburgh, and whoever was in charge of light entertainment in Manchester were all asking us to write material for them, instead of our submitting it hopefully and enclosing stamped, addressed envelopes. We were earning three, sometimes four, guineas a number; which of course had to be split between us. I think the Corporation must have worked out that it would be cheaper to get me on the staff; at any rate, in 1936 I was offered a job as a script-writer in the Variety Department in London under Eric Maschwitz at £250 a year, which I accepted even before reading the small print on the back of the offer. We were, I felt, in.

We were, but not really in the way I had expected. I did a three-months training course, learning which side of the microphone was live, and how by pounding two coconut shells together in slightly different ways they could sound like (a) Dick Turpin's ride to York or (b) the Grand National. I sat at a little desk surrounded by potentially distinguished alumni: John Ellison, Cecil McGivern, that gifted and lovable Irish dramatist Denis Johnson, David Lloyd-James, and Wynford Vaughan Thomas (who now, poor soul, is with Harlech in which I, poor soul, have shares). We listened or dozed through long and remarkably boring lectures on Balance and Control, the Function of the B.B.C.'s Engineering Division, and News-Reading Technique; but every now and then we were allowed to produce shows which were recorded and played back to the class for polite or acrimonious dissection. Denis Johnson and I did a full-length documentary on widgets; it was an outrageous send-up of the sort of documentary the B.B.C. did a lot of in those days, tracing the manufacture of widgets from the early smelting-down process to the finished article. We interviewed a number of widget-smelters, widget-welders, widget-furnacemen and widget-polishers, and even one or two of these gentlemen's wives and dependants, getting their views on the widget industry and ending up at the docks showing the vital and valuable export of millions of tons of British-made widgets. The whole programme was redolent with sound effects and heavy symbolic industrial music. It was taken completely seriously, even by the training-school instructors; after the play-back and post mortem Denis and I went round to the George in Mortimer Street and Denis said, "What d'you suppose a widget *is*?"

Large sections of the British public seem to be remarkably gullible. In recent years there have been healthy signs of distrust and cynicism seeping through, but until a few years ago if something was heard on the B.B.C. (even, as in the case of the widgets, on closed circuit), it was accepted as the gospel truth. "It must be right: I heard it on the B.B.C." Some years ago, in a television series called "A to Z", I did a take-off of those Horlicks strip-cartoon advertisements. In the first scene, I was really in a very bad way: unable to sleep, totally lacking in self-confidence, worried stiff in case Tom Sloan (Head of Light Entertainment, B.B.C. T.V.) would declare me redundant. (There was a certain degree of truth in this last anxiety.) In the second scene, I was being advised by my doctor (the late Ian Fleming, naturally; in those days he played all the doctors) that I was suffering from follicle starvation and the only thing to do was to take Umbrage. In the following scene, I was seen sitting up in bed drinking a large beaker of steaming hot Umbrage, with a tin of the product on my bedside table, the label facing the camera. The ensuing scenes showed the remarkable results of taking Umbrage. With the aid of some skilful trick camera work, I beat Christopher Chataway's four-minute mile record with consummate ease, broke the Olympic record for the one hundred metre crawl stroke, beat Joe Davis hands down at snooker, holed out in one at a 440-yarder, scored six or more consecutive bull's-eyes at darts, and accomplished various other similar feats of derring-do. The final shot showed me, abominably fit and healthy and now sleeping like a top, having heard from Mr. Sloan that my contract with the B.B.C. had been renewed in perpetuity at a vastly increased honorarium; there was a bubble coming out of one of my ears reading, *"Thinks*: I'm on top of the world thanks to taking Umbrage." On the morning following the programme, the chemists of this sceptred isle were inundated with demands for Umbrage. The manager of my local Boots told me that one of his assistants, according to him a nice and intelligent girl, had come to him practically with tears in her eyes saying she had another old lady on her hands screaming for the large-size tin, and why didn't they have any in stock? After all, it had been on the B.B.C. the night before.

Not only God moves in a mysterious way His wonders to perform. The B.B.C. is pretty good at this, too. Having been taken on as a script-writer in the Variety Department in London, at the end of the training course I was sent as Features and Drama producer to Aberdeen, replacing the aforesaid Moultrie Kelsall, who was moving on to pastures new. This was a blow; though, as things turned out, Aberdeen provided me with just about the happiest year-and-a-half of my life. But I was just beginning to get the feel and excitement of London; I was still raw enough to goggle at the lights in Piccadilly Circus and to think I was really living it up listening to Don Carlos and his Gipsy Balalaika Orchestra playing near-Dvorak while I ate gammon steak and drank a lager in Lyons' Corner House in Coventry Street. And there were still three, if not four, shows I hadn't yet seen from the gallery. There were two initial snags about the Aberdeen job. One was following in Moultrie's footsteps. He had been in charge of the station for several years and was much more than just its boss; he was God. The locals practically doffed their caps or curtsied when passing him in Union Street. The idea of a young whipper-snapper from London, of all places, taking over from him was unthinkable, even though I wisely played down the "from London" label and played up the "born-on-the-right-side-of-the-Tweed" gambit. (Can you play labels down and gambits up? I doubt it, but you know what I mean.) I didn't mention that the event had taken place only some two or three hundred yards on the "right" side, and even so had still been firmly in England. The other snag was the language problem. Especially in the country districts, the people of that north-east corner of Scotland speak not only with a very pronounced accent but use a great many words—mostly of Scandinavian origin—which are theirs and no-one else's. The afternoon I arrived in Aberdeen I was whisked straight from the station to the studios, which were then in a somewhat tumble-down ex-warehouse in Belmont Street. "Studios", perhaps, gives a false impression; there were two, one a boot-cupboard where we did talks, the fat stock prices, the epilogues, and so on; the other about the size of a large sitting-room, from whence came everything else, including massed choirs and brass bands, which fitted tightly and—as there was no ventilation—gave rise to body odour, especially among the contraltos and trombonists. I was introduced to some half-dozen of the regular broadcasters in the larger studio, where a hive of activity was going on which stopped abruptly on my arrival. They all studied me intently for a minute or two, and then Moultrie said, "Now, what animal *could* he be?" It transpired that their Children's Hour programme was going on the air in about half-an-hour and in their Children's Hour all the permanent participants were animals: the Aberdeen Animals. Moultrie was Brer Rabbit, Howard Lockhart was Howard the Hare, there was Miss Mouse and several others. Ruby Duncan (Mrs. Kelsall in what private life she had, which was practically nil) looked me up and down very seriously for about a couple of minutes and then said, "Mr. Mole." I didn't consider it at all flattering, but the proposal was adopted unanimously and Mr. Mole I remained in the Children's Hour programmes throughout my stay in Aberdeen. They asked me what was my best key, which always rather un-nerves me; the keys I know anything about are the front-door one and the ignition key of my car, and when I said, "Where's the script?" they all nearly passed out laughing. They were still laughing when the red light went on and we were on the air. We did a one-hour programme at least three afternoons a week, sometimes more, making the whole thing up as we went along and getting away—it seemed to me when I could hardly believe I had actually heard some of the Kelsall double entendres—with murder. In signing off each programme for the kiddie-winks, Moultrie had the frightening habit of saying, in his cosiest and friendliest voice, "Good-night, children . . . good-night" and then adding, the instant the red light in the studio went out, ". . . you fucking little bastards." I was convinced that one day he would be caught out and the message would get through to the juvs and their doting parents, but he never was.

If my first afternoon in the Aberdeen studios was to say the least breathless, the evening of the same day was nerve-racking. They were rehearsing what is known in those parts as a "bothy" entertainment: folk songs and dance music of the North-East, held very loosely together (sometimes, in fact, not held but dropped) by a vague kind of story-line, with a great deal of fiddling and accordion-playing. There was a large cast and Moultrie thought it would be an excellent idea if I stood in and got to know the regulars. I listened to a complete run-through of the show and didn't understand a word from start to finish. They might, for all I knew, have been speaking Hindustani. In the break we all trooped across to Mother Cameron's pub opposite the B.B.C. building, and I said to one of the stalwarts—a remarkable old boy called Arthur Black—"Quite a large cast, isn't it?" It wasn't a particularly witty remark but up to then I hadn't uttered, and I didn't want them to think that their new producer not only looked dumb, but was. "Aye, aye," said Mr. Black. "There's a gey boorachie o' fowk." Which, in a rough translation, meant that there was quite a sizeable collection of personnel. This was the last straw. I went to Moultrie and told him firmly that I could not be expected to produce a gang of foreigners when I didn't understand one word of their patois. He made some sympathetic, not-to-worry reply; but as this was also delivered in the vernacular, I didn't understand that either. Within three weeks, I was talking with as broad an accent as any of them, and words like "boorachie" were dropping from my lips like ninepins.

Aberdeen in those days was a remarkable little station. It was virtually a one-man show; you thought nothing of doing the routine office work all day—casting, contracts, and so on—with occasional interruptions to read the fat stock prices or introduce some speaker or piano recital; rehearse or produce a show in the evening; totter back from Mother Cameron's to read the Epilogue; switch off and lock up and go home with the keys of the joint. The output was phenomenal and its contents surprising. Moultrie was a jazz addict, and so am I; he had inaugurated a fortnightly programme called 'Facets of Syncopation', which against all opposition (both inside and outside the B.B.C.) I was determined to maintain. For one thing, I liked it. "Surely," the Aberdeen *Press and Journal* thundered, "it is the function of our local station to reflect the character, the arts and crafts and individuality of the region, rather than devote valuable time to the melancholy wailings and boop-a-doopings of New Orleans. Can there be anyone here in Aberdeenshire who genuinely enjoys this drivel?" There was; the kids lapped it up. So, I suspect, did a good many of the oldies. There was the most incredible reservoir of talent to call on. Almost all of it was semi-professional. They did their daytime chores—schoolteachers, commercial travellers, tailors, one or two farmers and fishermen—and came to the studios around 6.30 and got down to the other side of their lives. Ruby Duncan and her partner, a pawky schoolmaster called Jimmy Ross, were the best pair of syncopated pianists I have ever heard; there was a thrilling sort of rapport between them; sitting facing each other at the two grand pianos one would raise an eyebrow or the other would give a little nod at the end of a phrase, and you knew it had been mutely decided what magic or mischief was coming next. I was more than delighted when, years later, I found the adorable Mrs. Kelsall as one of the two pianists in the orchestra pit at an intimate revue of mine in the West End. There were two brothers—farm-labourers near Strachan, a few miles north of Aberdeen—who played the trumpet and trombone like angels; one joined Ted Heath and the other, I think, Joe Loss. But they just came in in the evenings, often still in their working clothes and with a fair amount of shit on their boots, and played for the hell of it. Plus, I must admit, three guineas a show; which was about as high as we could go in those days. And there was Blondie. I have forgotten her real name; another one up to Sir Compton. She sang blues better than anyone I have ever heard, save Sinatra. And in the morning she went back to serve behind the counter in one of the local stores, praying for her next B.B.C. engagement. We did intimate (and rather risqué) revues, heavy historical dramas and light comedies, documentaries galore (I was sick for three days on a trawler for a herring epic called 'Landings at Lossiemouth'), serious music, musical comedy, quizzes, the lot. We interviewed anyone who was in the news, and many who just wanted to be. Once I took the portable recorder and microphone to Harold Fraser-Simson, the composer of 'The Maid of the Mountains', in the dank castle he lived in near Inverness. We were sitting in front of an inadequate log fire in his drawing-room when he suddenly upped from his armchair, went over to the grand piano, and said, "They've *never* played 'Love Will Find A Way' *right*. They bugger it up like this"—he played it sharply, staccato—"and I wrote it like *this*" and he played it lovingly and legato and then went back to his arm-chair, having at last got the whole thing out of his system. I ran a monthly sort of magazine programme called, of all unfortunate titles, 'Queeries'; it consisted of half-a-dozen five-minute talks by people who had peculiar jobs or had had un-usual experiences. One day an extremely tough Aberdonian called Jock Bruce came to see me, saying he had a story that he thought might interest me. He certainly had; he had been, he said, with Lawrence of Arabia through most of the desert campaign and had stayed with him in his R.A.F. days when that strange, muddled character became Aircraftsman Shaw. He had had to carry out—against, he insisted, his better judgment—the things that Lawrence required from a master. I gave him five minutes on the show; naturally it hit the front pages. What still worries me is that Bruce gave me a forty-thousand-word manuscript in his own tiny, scrawling handwriting about his relationship and experiences with Law-rence. I kept it for some time but I couldn't decide whether he was true or phoney, or a bit of both; in the end I did noth-ing about it. He has cropped up again fairly recently in the Sundays; they don't seem able to make up their minds about him either.

Aberdeen was fun; certainly until we moved into much grander premises which were actually called Broadcasting House. The station was raised somewhat in status and some-one called the Aberdeen Representative was grafted on to us. He was a delightful old gentleman who was on the verge of retiring from the B.B.C.; he had an absolute horror of programmes, especially some of the kind of programmes we had been putting out. His argument was that the fewer pro-grammes you put out, the less chance there was of any trouble. His policy seems to have been continued even after he re-tired; they certainly seem to do very little, compared with our output, up there nowadays. Pity, I am sure there is the same exciting talent there now as there was in my day. Perhaps even—behind some shop counter—another Blondie, waiting.

Towards the end of 1938 I was posted to a better, or at least a better-paid, position with the B.B.C. in Glasgow. This was not nearly such fun as Aberdeen, mainly because the B.B.C. in Glasgow was bigger; in Aberdeen, at any rate until the arrival of the Representative, you were more or less on your own; in Glasgow you were answerable to Programme Directors and Regional Controllers and weekly programme board meetings and all that jazz The chances of war even then seemed fifty-fifty, if not odds on. Auntie, planning ahead as always (it is an odd thing that the B.B.C. plans ahead, has a fetish about anniversaries, but somehow misses out on the present) was busily engaged getting everything set up, just in case; in addition to my routine duties as a producer, I was liaised to the Outside Broadcasts division. This was run by an incredible character called Peter Keith Murray. He plunged into the preparations for covering the holocaust with the most infectious enthusiasm and zeal; I think if war had not been declared he would have committed suicide. Much of the planning took place late at night in a rather sleazy night-club in Sauchiehall Street; Peter had a ginger military moustache and midway through explaining, by diagrams drawn on the table-cloth (which he took home with him, also just in case) or by moving his fourth or fifth pink gin, that in the event of hostilities we would have an Outside Broadcast van *there*, three portable tape-recorders *here*, and *here*, and reliable contacts on the phone at points A, B, C and D, he would break off and stroke the ends of his moustache when something delectable passed the table and say, "I say, old boy, not a bad-looking saddle of crumpet, eh?" When the—I suppose —inevitable happened and war did break out, the first enemy bomb was dropped on the Forth Bridge. Well, not on; it missed by a good quarter-of-a-mile. The Scottish Regional

Outside Broadcasts War Reporting Unit (Peter, myself, and a recording engineer called Cyril) was based on Glasgow. We tore at seventy miles or more to Queensferry, where I recorded a graphic reconstruction of this world-shattering event for the national news. I described the bridge; I said that it reached across the Firth of Forth from South Queensferry on the south side of the river to North Queensferry on the north side. I said that if the bomb had been dropped south of the bridge, it must have come down somewhere roughly about *there*; if on the other hand, as some eye-witness maintained, it had fallen north of the bridge, it would in all probability have come down roughly about *there*. I said that the eye-witnesses whom I had just interviewed (I hadn't) had said that the aircraft had come in very low, or comparatively low, or moderately high, and that until the bomb was dropped they had had no reason to suspect that this was, in fact, the first enemy air attack on our country. I stressed the importance of the Forth Bridge as a vital communication link between England and Scotland; this was cut out of the recording in case it gave away valuable information to the Germans. (I had a feeling they must have known about the link or they wouldn't have come over in such a hurry and tried to bomb it.) I ended rather weakly, I remember, by saying that if in actual fact a bomb had actually been dropped either north or south of the bridge, it must by now be down there somewhere.

It must without doubt have been the greatest job of non-reporting the B.B.C. put across in the whole war.

3

AFTER THE bomb, absolutely nothing happened in the war in Scotland until poor Hess dropped in, by which time I had been transferred back to London and had joined the B.B.C.'s North American Service. The Corporation had been carved up into three categories, A, B and C; if you were A, which for some odd reason I was, you were classified as essential and not allowed to join up. The North American Service was, though you were forbidden to use the dirty word, propaganda; America was not yet in the war, and indeed seemed to be showing a marked reluctance to become involved; our job was to impress the United States, via Canada, just how serious things were and how gallantly Britain was Taking It. Of all ridiculous expressions; we had precious little alternative. Because of the regrettable difference in time between the United States and ourselves, we went on the air at eleven p.m. and operated until dawn, transmitting mainly from what until then had been the basement of C. and A.'s in Oxford Street. All sorts of famous people managed somehow to get to the basement through the blitz and were bedded down in camp beds and wakened with cups of tea shortly before two a.m. and four a.m., which were the two main propaganda talks spots in the programme; they then went blearily to the studio and told the Americans how splendidly we were all behaving, managing subtly to suggest that by staying out of the war they were really missing a ball. The same exercise was going on non-stop from Bush House, the propaganda there being directed then, as now, to the Middle and Far East. A very brisk, extremely clean-shaven and talced new boy called Norman Collins had joined our unit; it was part of my duties to enlighten him on how to deal with these distinguished speakers, put them at their ease, get their scripts down to the right length (14 mins, 45 secs) without appearing to cut any of their favourite purple patches, send out for cups of coffee or aspirins, and so on. I was impressed by the way he buckled down to work. He never seemed to stop writing at his little desk opposite mine in the basement; later I found that what he was writing was a monumentally successful novel called *London Belongs To Me*. One of the regular broadcasters in the small hours—as well as doing a highly popular fifteen-minute talk on Sunday nights on the Home Service—was J. B. Priestley. Mr. Priestley is a dear man, but needs cosseting. He needed, in fact, a Scotch or two before doing his stuff at four in the morning, and who could blame him? The first time he appeared in the basement during Norman Collins' term of office, Norman greeted him with, "Hullo, Jack!" The rest of us were appalled; we had always called Mr. Priestley Mr. Priestley, and when I shook him awake in his little camp bed, I used to say, "I'm afraid it's time, sir." Mr. Priestley said, "Hullo, Norman, good to see you," which put us all in perspective. Collins, I know, wanted to become the B.B.C.'s Director-General, and almost did; he also, I think, wanted to be Prime Minister, and may still want to. I met him once in Bond Street and he said, "Come and help me choose a watch; it's my wedding anniversary tomorrow and I want to give the missus a little something. Nothing ostentatious," he added to the assistant. "Around the two-fifty mark." He would have made an even worse Prime Minister than some who had better remain anonymous; he might have made rather a good D.-G. He was ruthlessly ambitious; he wouldn't have wasted time charming birds off trees, but he would have used his undoubted charming capabilities to get exactly what he wanted, irrespective of who was hurt; and perhaps nowadays, coping with commercial opposition, this is what the B.B.C. needs at the mast-head instead of well-mannered tea-cosies.

In an unguarded moment, I suggested to the Powers that Be that it might not be a bad idea to put out on the North American Service a daily soap-opera about an ordinary London family Taking It. The Powers, after some dithering, agreed and said I could have a go for six weeks only, and to watch the budget. This was a show called initially, 'Front Line Family', later re-named, 'The Robinson Family'; it went out six days a week for six years and was, one has to admit, the fore-runner of the Groves, the Dales, the Archers, and all the rest of them. I had one secretary, and a very excellent one, too; how she coped and remained calm I cannot think. I rehearsed and recorded one episode each morning; we did the office work—casting, correspondence, all those tiresome details you have to fill in when you've used eighteen seconds of Eric Coates' 'Knightsbridge March' as a signature tune, and the returns have to go to the Performing Right Society—and I wrote another episode every evening. Six days a week for a year and a half; after which I decided I was all for the quiet life and—category A or no category A—resigned from the B.B.C. and joined the R.A.F. There was no difficulty in getting actors; all the theatres in London had closed down except the Windmill . . . and, later, to one's joy, Wyndhams, where the curtain rose rather tentatively at four o'clock in the afternoon (because of the black-out) on a Herbert Farjeon miscellany called *Diversion*, and life, in spite of the blitz, seemed to have miraculously started up again. I saw it eight times. The cast included such diverse talent as Bernard Miles, Walter Crisham and Dame Edith Evans; and just to see footlights lit again and listen to laughter in a theatre was magic.

In 'Front Line Family' we had a small permanent company; Dulcie Gray as the love interest, Ernest Butcher and a little-known but excellent Scottish character actress called Nell Ballantyne as the Taking-It's father and mother; for guest appearances we just had to ring up and the stars or near-stars, many of whom had not worked since war broke out, came flocking. Nell had been living happily and peacefully in semi-retirement in Scotland; I knew what a good actress she was, and she had exactly the sort of soft, dark brown lilt to her voice that I knew would get our transatlantic cousins. I wrote to her outlining the plans for the serial and asking her if she'd be interested, telling her to think the whole thing over very carefully, because it was a serious step to take; the show might be a flop and in any case London was not a nice place to live in. I got a telegram by return reading, "Try to stop me", and she was on the B.B.C.'s doorstep within twenty-four hours carrying a large suitcase and saying, "I'm here, dear".

She, and the rest of the regulars in the show, behaved impeccably; there was never a sign of temperament, and this in a way was understandable. Each episode ended with a cliff-hanger; usually a bomb coming down on what was obviously going to be a direct hit on the Robinson's house (it wasn't), or the news that Mrs. Robinson's sister's semi-detached had been hit by an incendiary and was a raging inferno with Mrs. Robinson's sister trapped in an upstairs bedroom or that young Andy Robinson in Fighter Command has been reported shot down over enemy territory . . . and the cast knew that if there was the slightest trouble I could wipe any or all of them off in the next instalment, or in the case of poor Andy make him a prisoner of war for the next six months or longer, with some other actor or actress reading the few letters the poor boy was allowed to send home. I have never wielded such potential power. I must say this arrangement worked amicably both ways; if Dulcie wanted a couple of months off for a theatre engagement when these began cropping up again, I just made her pregnant. The amazing thing was how people all over the world (the serial started on the North American Service only, but later was heard on all the other B.B.C. Overseas Services as well as in this country) took it for *real*; they seemed to think that in some strange way a microphone had been sneaked into a real house belonging to a real family in London and that everything they heard was actually happening. When Dulcie—or rather the character she was playing—did become pregnant, it almost seemed that half the female population of the British Commonwealth and a great many dear, good, blue-rinsed matrons in Moose Lake, Minnesota, or Doylestown, Pasadena, got out their knitting-needles in order to ply us with little woollies. Nell Ballantyne had a sort of catch-phrase which ran through the epic; in whatever drama or disaster she found herself—and God knows she found herself in many, usually six a week—she would say, "What I'd give for a nice cup of tea". Tea poured in from all over the world; so much so that Ernest Butcher one day suggested to me that I might make him say, even if only occasionally, "What I'd give for a nice nip of Scotch". It was, so far as I know, the first example in this country of the grip a regular show on radio or television can have on the listener or viewer; if you put the same group of characters in the same locale and in permutations of the same situations, the customers are hooked. Especially if, as in our case, you do it daily. However terrible the show may be, you get them. Take, for example, nowadays—no, let us be charitable, if only for dear Violet Carson's sake. She was nice to me in the North Region's Children's Hour.

I have to admit that the serial was not so popular with the forces serving overseas. Some time after I left it and was temporarily working (or idling) as a P.R.O. at the Air Ministry, I had to meet a senior R.A.F. officer who had just come back from the Middle East, where he had been checking up on the chaps' morale. "I'll tell you something," he said to me, his moustache bristling. "There's one thing that causes more resentment and ill-feeling and general lowering of morale than anything else the B.B.C. puts out. I don't know if you've ever heard of it, dear boy, but it's the most god-awful, sloppy, sentimental dose of crap called 'Front Line Family', and if you can do anything to get the damn thing stopped you'd be doing something *really* useful instead of just sitting there." "Really, sir?" I said. "I'll make a note of that." I thought it wiser not to tell him I had started the whole thing.

In those days one moved house a good deal; one had to. Flats in London were easy to find but liable to disappear overnight. To begin with, I took a bedsitter in Hallam Street which was convenient both for the canteen in Broadcasting House and the basement in Oxford Street. Before clocking in for the start of each night's eleven p.m. session, I used to have a drink in a friendly pub just round the corner from Broadcasting House. I went there as usual one night when there was a fairly heavy blitz on; the pub was moderately full and the guv'nor and his missus were behind the bar, worried because it was getting near closing time and their teenage son was at some late-night classes at the Polytechnic in Regent Street and hadn't come home. I found I had come out without any money; the guv'nor, who by this time knew me as a regular imbiber, said not to worry, mate, settle up tomorrow night, and did I want to borrow a quid. For some reason, I insisted on going back to the bed-sitter in Hallam Street and collecting some cash. While I was doing so something came down too close to be comfortable. When I went back round the corner, the pub wasn't there. Everyone in it was killed; I kept thinking of the son coming home from the Polytechnic and finding it looking like that.

When the daily production of 'Front Line Family' was switched to the B.B.C.'s studios in Maida Vale, Dulcie, Nell and I took a furnished flat nearby in Warwick Avenue. The girls looked after the flat, did the shopping (Nell, being Scots, was better with coupons than Dulcie) and cooked my supper while I churned out the next instalment of the serial. It was, they said, their war work and the least they could do; during supper they put out tentative feelers about what was going to happen to their characters after that unexploded mine blew them all sky-high at the end of episode 286. At around two o'clock one morning the phone rang and a rather agitated voice said there had been a direct hit on the Maida Vale studios and the night duty-officer thought I ought to know. I flung on some clothes and raced down to find that the fire brigade had caused more damage than the Nazis and the place was awash. We recorded the show three weeks in advance of transmission date, and somewhere in the building there were eighteen tapes of the opus. I stood in a long corridor in the basement with the water up to my knees and cardboard boxes containing tapes swirling past; I snatched them up and read the labels, if the labels were still on. If it was Eric Robinson or Vera Lynn they were flung straight back in the water; if it was 'Front Line Family' they were grabbed and subsequently dried out. By the most fabulous work by the B.B.C. engineers, we were able to record the daily instalment of the serial the morning after the studios had been hit. It seems strange to think of it, but when that episode was broadcast listeners wrote in from Canada and Australia asking why they had heard some rather pizzicato plonkings in the background. The reason was a simple one: the roof of the studio had been badly damaged, it was pouring with rain, and we put down the big copper tubs the B.B.C. provide as ash-trays at all strategic positions on the studio floor to catch the drips.

Because of bombs, transport difficulties and the uncertainty of artists turning up on time if at all, many of the B.B.C. departments, both home and overseas, had been partly if not wholly evacuated; like the kids who left London, some bewildered and crying, some excited and giggling, with their names and to them unknown future addresses printed on labels tied in the button-holes of their coats. A large section of the Variety Department emigrated to North Wales, giving rise (no doubt with reason) to the impassioned cri de coeur from an outraged Welsh pastor, "There's buggery in Bangor!" Part of the North American Service, myself included, went for a time to Abbey Manor, a large and draughty stately home which the Corporation had annexed just outside Evesham. I bought a second- or eighth-hand Ford for £7. 10s. 0d., packed what seemed essential into it, and set out for the tranquil life in the Vale. I gave a lift to Georgie Henschel, who was the daughter of the distinguished musician Sir George Henschel and was one of the announcers and continuity girls on the North American Service; she said she had got everything planned and had done a recce and found a delightful farm-house only a few miles from Evesham and she would look after us and have scrumptious brekker waiting for us when we came home worn out after our all-night chores. She looked on it, she added, as part of her war work and the least she could do. All the girls seemed to be saying that in those days. John Ellison, Robert Dougal, Bob Beatty and I fell all too readily for this arrangement, discovering very quickly that the dear girl couldn't so much as boil an egg. We spent all our spare time cooking for her and going round the farm-house not with a vacuum cleaner, but with a very ancient and wheezy sweeper which rejected anything as unimportant as fluff and cigarette ash and got its works (or what was left of them) clogged up on anything larger. John Ellison had a motor-bike of which he was not the complete master; he rides horses more than capably but the technique of riding motor-bikes seems to have escaped him. Once when the Ford was *hors de combat*, as frequently happened, he offered me a lift back to the farm-house when we came off duty shortly after five in the morning. He placed

65

the motor-bike in the middle of Evesham High Street, facing in the right direction; he had to do this, being not very good at cornering. I was just about to lower myself on to the pillion seat when, quite unexpectedly and as the result of an agitated jab on the starter by John's right foot, the engine started up and John and the bike disappeared at about fifty miles an hour down the High Street and out of sight, making a great deal of noise and flushing a lot of wild-fowl. I was left in the middle of the High Street with my legs bowed like a cowboy in a Western, and, as John had not got the knack of stopping the machine unless it ran into a haystack near the entrance to the farm-house or up a steep grass bank on arriving at Abbey Manor, let alone mastered the art of reversing, I walked back to the farm and arrived just in time to take Miss Henschel's breakfast up to her room.

George Inns, the one man who has proved that apartheid can be hearty (he is, of course, the genius behind the Black and White Minstrels) was another evacuee to Abbey Manor. He was, and is, the most terrible giggler and an acknowledged expert in making others giggle in the most sombre circumstances. The so-called studios in the stately home were, naturally, fit-up jobs; the experts had done their best about accoustics, but their best consisted of hanging drapes round the walls of what had obviously in the grand old days been a guest bedroom or, in one case, a bathroom which we used for any programmes where we felt a bit of echo might help. In addition to our other chores, John, Bob and I took turns in reading the news, which in those days was invariably grim. I would be halfway through a depressing catalogue of calamities—H.M.S. so-and-so torpedoed with no known survivors, another all-night raid on Coventry or Liverpool, Mr. Churchill telling us we had our backs to the wall, our shoulders to the wheel, and our more important parts—our fronts —completely open to enemy attack and obviously in a very dicey position; midway through the catalogue the curtains facing me would bulge outwards in my direction and George would appear making funny faces and wiggling his ears, which he was rather good at. He could wiggle one while the other remained static, which is an unusual accomplishment. I feel Derek Nimmo should try it and abandon that toes routine. I used to end up the list of disasters hysterical with laughter; I only hope the listeners thought it was interference, which it certainly was.[1]

After some four hundred or more episodes of 'Front Line Family', I resigned, as I say, from the B.B.C. and informed the R.A.F. that I was available and ready to bring the war to a swift conclusion, one way or the other. It wasn't any sudden outburst of patriotism or an intense desire to take part in the actual fighting; if you lived in London in those days you were, I suppose as close to the front line as anywhere. You over-acted a bit but, on the whole, behaved well. I have a theory that there are two things that bring out the best in us —war and snow. Along my terrace, if we have an unexpected snow-storm, we are out at once, shovelling away the snow from not only our own but our next-door neighbours' front passages and saying, 'No trouble at all; leave it to me, dear.' The moment the thaw sets in, we stop talking to each other. The same happens as soon as we start fighting; we behave beautifully. But we certainly over-act; I remember walking down Shaftesbury Avenue one morning. It was a glorious day with not a cloud in the sky, and not a siren had sounded. But something and someone was up there, and there was the slow, gradual, ominous drone of a bomb coming down, and clearly coming down adjacent. I took complete control of the situation. "Lie down," I shouted. "Lie *flat*!" The bomb landed just round the corner, at the top of Berwick Market. When we all picked ourselves up and dusted ourselves down, I realized that I had commanded the passing pedestrians to flatten them-

[1] George, alas, died in July, 1970.

67

selves under the plate-glass awning of the Apollo Theatre.

Leaving the B.B.C. and joining up was, I suppose, a sort of guilt complex. People I knew would come home on leave and they would keep wearing uniform all through their leave; and I was in another sort of uniform—B.B.C. uniform. There were and still are two varieties of this : the neat clerical grey or pin-stripe with the white collar and old school tie for the administrative types, and for the creative people— especially those who in those days wrote very long documentaries in blank verse—absolutely filthy duffle coats and beer-stained corduroy trousers. Carnaby Street shirts and psychedelic ties have now been added to the creative sector's gear; the beer-stained cords remain. Sometimes, by the look of them, I think they must be the same cords handed down. But little remarks started to be made : "Still in the B.B.C., are you? Good job, I suppose; I mean, regular hours, able to sleep in your own bed, all that sort of thing." I couldn't stand it any longer; and I was getting a little tired of the regular hours which were working out at around eighteen a day.

To my amazement the R.A.F. recruiting officer I went to showed no enthusiasm at all when I offered my services. The whole thing, in fact, was a bit of an anti-climax. He took a languid note of my name, address, age and previous experience if any, and said disinterestedly that if something cropped up they would probably get in touch. I have seldom felt more deflated. I had imagined that within hours I would be in Fighter Command, if not actually up in a Spitfire pulverising the opposition, at least in some vital position at Fighter Command H.Q. saying things like "Control to Z.K. 109 : formation of thirty Messerschmidts reported two miles to starboard : over" or even just "Roger" like they keep saying nowadays over the inter-com in taxis. To replace me, the B.B.C. had engaged a lady script-writer who had, or said she had, considerable experience in American soap-opera; they had also taken on a producer for the serial, and quite a team of assistant producers, panel operators, effects boys, and heaven knows what else. Until then the whole show had been done by myself with the invaluable assistance of a young man called Ken Hughes, who worked the grams while I twiddled the knobs and did all the fades and cross-fades and so on. He is now a highly successful writer and film director, which does not surprise me in the least; he had enormous talent. The lady script-writer's scripts proved unacceptable to the B.B.C.; and as the Corporation had found that I had not been snatched up with alacrity by the R.A.F. and was still kicking my heels in London, they asked me to come back and take over the serial again until I was called up. I said I would do so on condition that I heard all the instalments recorded after I had left, and that if I didn't approve of them they would have to be destroyed and we would start all over again. I didn't approve of them (neither did the cast); they were destroyed; and the B.B.C. was faced with the bill for recording three weeks' episodes which ended up in the incinerator at Maida Vale. We all adjourned to the pub round the corner after the last of the three weeks' monstrosities went up in flames, and had quite a session.

After a month or two, however, the R.A.F. became suddenly alert to the gravity of the war situation, realised that they could no longer struggle on without people like myself, and I was summoned to the colours, kitted out in the pale blue ensemble and posted to Skegness to do my square-bashing. This was the spring of 1941, and very pleasant it was, too. Apart from bashing squares, we swam, played tennis, and slept or read paper-backs while a sad elderly corporal instructed us in the inner workings of the Winchester rifle. At the end of the square-bashing I was posted to a Bomber Command station in Lincolnshire where, with four or five others, I spent several months digging a trench. It was a very long trench and it was summer and we took our time over the job; the trench stretched across several fields and as neither end of it was connected to anything else, none of us—not even the other corporal in charge of the digging party—ever found out what it was in aid of. I have a feeling that the Adjutant of the Bomber Command station, finding himself with a posse of useless erks on his hands, just said, "Send them out and get them weaving digging a trench." I then went through a course in radar, midway through which, as a result of sleeping between filthy blankets, I contracted scabies which were falsely diagnosed as venereal disease and I was sent to quite the wrong hospital until the misunderstanding was sorted out. For a time I really thought I'd got it, except that I couldn't work out how and from whom. My last few sexual contacts had all seemed so clean and above-board. In spite of this rather disturbing incident, I ended up as an R.D.F.Op.—Radar Direction Finding Operator—and was all set to identify hostile or unfriendly aircraft on the radar screen and start doing my "Roger" act. I was posted to Benbecula, which is an island in the Outer Hebrides and just about as far as you can get from the British mainland without actually coming under the Fifth Amendment. It is a barren but beautiful island; because of the permanent gales, no trees grow there and you walk leaning forward at an angle of forty-five degrees, bent against the wind. Even when we got back on the mainland and were landed at Oban, after a terrible crossing with usually a great many cattle as fellow-passengers, we still walked at that angle until we realised that it was possible to remain upright without being bowled over. During the whole of the winter I spent on Benbecula, I never plotted a single enemy aircraft and no-one could blame them for keeping their distance from the place; I became quite expert, however, at tracking the progress of the N.A.A.F.I. wagon as it left the Coastal Command headquarters on the island and made its way to our radar outpost some two or three miles away with the mid-day meal of stewed beef and two tepid veg and stodgy spotted dick. And on one leave I made a very serious mistake. I spent part of the leave back in Berwick, staying with the doctor and his wife; also staying with them in the same colour of uniform as mine but rather better cut and embellished was someone who had married a younger sister of Mrs. Mclagan. His name was Sir Brian Baker, and he was Air Chief Marshal in charge of Coastal Command. "What are you doing, eh?" he asked. I said I was having a ball in his very own Command; I was on an island called Benbecula where nothing ever happened except a film show in the main hangar on alternate Thursday nights if the aircraft carrying the film had managed to land; I was trying to write a play, the plot of which up to then had eluded me; and apart from the gales and the stodgy spotted dick was having the time of my life. This was, of course, fatal. I had no sooner got back to Benbecula (the journey took two days) when I was told that I was once again posted, this time to the R.A.F. Officers' Training College in Calne (where, apart from embryo R.A.F. officers, the sausages come from) to be commissioned. Because of the time it took to get from the Outer Hebrides to Wiltshire, I was a day or two late in arriving for the commissioning course; as had happened on arriving late at Edinburgh Academy, all the beds round the walls in our sleeping-quarters had been commandeered and I was again left with the one in the middle. The sergeant showing me to the sleeping-quarters on the morning I arrived had somehow or other got to know that I had been mixed up with the B.B.C. "You'd know the C.O.," he said, pointing to a door on which was inscribed the billing, 'Squadron-Leader P. S. G. Waddington, Officer Commanding.' "He was in your sort of queer carry-on," the sergeant added. "Never heard of him," I said. When, an hour or so later, we were all whipped to attention while the C.O. strode down the centre aisle for our first lecture of the day, I realised that it was Patrick Waddington. He had been one-third of a successful musical act called That Certain Trio, and I had last seen him in Evesham High Street wearing a pale pink chiffon scarf and leading two borzois. He never acknowledged by so much of a flicker of an eyelash that our paths had crossed until the (literally) passing-out party at the end of the course. He said then that I must have thought him a bit stand-offish but it wasn't really on for the Commanding Officer to fraternise with the men. By some odd fluke, or perhaps due to the lack of any real competition, I passed out Head Cadet of the course. The reward for this honour was not riding that poor horse up all those steps as at Sandhurst, but acting as the officer in charge of the final passing-out parade in the presence of several lofty visitors from the Air Ministry and, of course, the Commanding Officer. I had such a raging hang-over from the party the night before that I couldn't remember what came next; only quick thinking and a stentorian yell of "about turn!" from a disapproving Warrant Officer stopped the entire platoon marching straight out of Wiltshire and into Somerset.

Before this, however—actually while I was digging the trench—I had received out of the blue a letter which I must have read at least fifteen times before even getting round to believing it. The London theatres were cautiously beginning to open up again and the one to follow Wyndham's was the Comedy in Panton Street; the letter said that an intimate revue—provisional title *Rise Above It*—was to be put on there and if I had any material which I thought might be suitable would I come to the theatre and ask for Walter Crisham, who was directing the show. I was due a forty-eight-hour pass in any case and belted down to London; if I hadn't been due leave I would still have gone and risked court-martial. I couldn't have been reduced to the ranks or at any rate no further reduced as I was still an A.C.2. I would just, I supposed, have got a month's solitary confinement or had either my spotted dick docked or the trench lengthened; it would certainly have been worth it.

In those days I was so ignorant of theatre ways (sometimes, especially at the Royal Court, I think I still am) that instead of going to the stage door of the Comedy I went in through the front of the house, past the box-office which hadn't yet opened up for business, and groped my way in the dark to somewhere around row S of what was then called the pit, and sat down, rather scared. The stage was lit by a single bare working light; the safety curtain was up and the entire company was assembled on-stage, sitting on hard wooden chairs and reading some sketch which obviously few of them cared for. It was pouring with rain outside (I had with me one of those unattractive capes which also serve as ground-sheets) and it was bitterly cold; all the mummers were huddled in coats or mackintoshes, and with their specs on the end of their noses, and stubbing out cigarette ends with their wellingtons they didn't really look all that glamorous. There were two ladies, one with one dog and the other with two, sitting as far as possible from each other, who seemed particularly acrimonious; on later introduction these proved to be Miss Hermione Gingold and Miss Hermione Baddeley. There was that dear man and good actor Henry Kendall, with a streaming cold, borrowing tissues. The director, Walter Crisham, was an amusing if acid American, who always looked as though he was about to say something libellous, and more often than not did. Some years later, when he was rehearsing for a straight play, the director handed out sheets of foolscap to the company at the first read-through and said he wanted all of them to write down their interpretation and evaluation of the parts they were playing. The motivation, the innermost feelings, the psychological background, the fears and hopes and stresses and ambitions of each character in the play as the actor or actress portraying that character saw them. Only through doing this, the director explained, could a cast really get *inside* the play they were appearing in, could *feel* it, be a *part* of it, make the whole concept a

73

living and fundamental *entity*. Mr. Crisham turned to whoever was sitting next to him and said, in a voice just loud enough for the director to hear, "How d'you spell 'shit'?"

This—sitting in or around row S and gaping open-mouthed at the scene on that bare stage—was my first experience of the professional theatre. It did not last long. The rehearsal pianist sighted me, left her piano in the orchestra pit and came striding up the centre aisle. She was a tall lady of regal aspect called Hero de Rance; she still obliges in the orchestra pit, often—especially if she has friends out front—giving more vivacious performances than the actors on the stage. She said, or rather hissed at me, "Don't you realise this is a private rehearsal? Get out this instant!" I was so taken aback that I got out at once, back into Panton Street and the pouring rain. I put my cape on and thought, this is ridiculous. After all, they asked me to come and see them. I walked round the block once or twice, getting steadily moister, and then saw a little slit in the wall at the rear of the theatre with the magic sign 'Stage Door' above it. Well, it can be magic; on the last night of a short run it rarely seems so. And in I went. Miss Gingold, Miss Baddeley and Mr. Crisham were in the middle of a blazing row when I was shown on stage; Mr. Kendall, between sneezes, was pitching in provocative insults from the side-line whenever the argument showed signs of petering out. However, they broke off shouting at each other as soon as I appeared and were all very charming. I think they were relieved to see a new face, even one like mine; and both Miss Gingold and Miss Baddeley were susceptible to uniform. Miss Gingold's taste ran more to navy blue and bell-bottom trousers, preferably worn tightly by Americans; Miss Baddeley seemed to have no preference at all in the three colour schemes available at the time, but preferred uniforms with rather more braid and decorations that I had on mine; but I suppose at a morning rehearsal in a bitterly cold theatre on a pouring wet Monday even an A.C.2 made a welcome change.

I had brought some of my wares with me. There was the usual embarrassing stillness while Walter Crisham flicked through some of the scripts; once he gave the tiniest move on one side of his mouth which could have signified nausea or might have been the hasty suppression of a premature or ill-timed smile. After what seemed an eternity he turned to me and said, "Not bad, kid. Not at all bad." "They couldn't be worse than the crap we've just read," said Miss Baddeley with one of her baby-doll moues. "Who wrote *that*, for God's sake?" Miss Gingold said, "I did, darling," and all three dogs bared their teeth and snarled at the opposition kennels, dead on cue. "Mind if I keep these?" said Mr. Crisham. "Can't promise anything, but you never know. The guy who's putting up the dough has to read all the material and the trouble with him—or one of the troubles—is he can't read. If you got any more stuff, send it along, honey. 'Bye for now." As I left they were deciding to take a coffee break and Miss Baddeley was saying, "*Coffee*? what mummy wants isn't coffee but a very large brandy-boo, isn't that what mummy wants, my precious?" She was talking to one of her dogs, not to Miss Gingold.

Although I saw very little of it, being still engaged on important war work (digging the trench) *Rise Above It* was a big success, running in its two editions for just under four hundred performances. And my name was at last in a theatre programme; even, though in extremely small print, on the bills outside the theatre. It was a bright, gay little show, occasionally witty and occasionally outrageous; together or separately the four stars worked like beavers and were capably backed by a small but talented company of youngsters. At the end of one performance a very large rat came out of the prompt side stage box and walked slowly along the footlights as the company were taking their curtain calls. The results were intriguing. As the troupe kept on bowing and grimacing to the applause, each in turn caught sight of the rat and reacted in various ways. Miss Gingold got up on a chair which had been left on stage from the finale and hoisted her skirt; Miss Baddeley just walked off stage and across to the pub opposite and had one. The audience, at least those in the stalls, were unable to see the rat; they thought it was all part of the show, and went on applauding. Hero de Rance, sensing that something was amiss, stood up in the orchestra pit, looked over the footlights, and found herself face to face with the rat who by this time had tired of the company and had turned round to look out front. Miss de Rance put one leg over the brass rail of the orchestra pit in an attempt to exit, and then turned very queasy indeed and remained in that position for some time. It was quite a night.

The great thing for me was that *Rise Above It* was the start of a long association with that talented, if at times tricky, quartette—Gingold, Baddeley, Kendall and Crisham; and through them an entrance to the theatre generally. I have often wondered what might have happened, or not happened, if I hadn't put on my cape in the pouring rain in Panton Street that morning, walked round the block, and found the stage door.

Rise Above It was followed by *Sweet and Low* at the Ambassadors and in that and the two subsequent revues—*Sweeter and Lower* and *Sweetest and Lowest*—I was almost unbelievably lucky in being either on the spot or with spare time to write while the shows were going through the periods of planning and collecting material. When the labour pains were on for *Sweet and Low* I was stationed at the Air Ministry and living in the flat I had leased in Grape Street; when we were on heat for *Sweeter and Lower* I was certainly not on the spot—I was, in fact, in a tent in Normandy—but there was a lull in the fighting and I wrote most of the show out there. And when *Sweetest and Lowest* was being conceived, I was back in London waiting to be sent out to the Far East.

The tent where a great deal of *Sweeter and Lower* was written was in a permanently mist-bound swamp a few miles south of Caen, obviously carefully chosen by the recce officer who had preceded its pitching, and surrounded by what seemed and sounded like several million randy bull-frogs. There were two camp beds in the tent and the one opposite mine was occupied by the late and much lamented Arthur Macrae, who was also engaged on vital war work. He was writing a musical called *Under the Counter* for Cicely Courtneidge. I imagine it must have been one of the comparatively rare occasions when two West End hits were being written in the same small tent by two R.A.F. officers alleged to be assisting in the liberation of Europe. It cannot be a thing that happens often; sometimes it amazes me that we won the war. I suppose the others just got on with it; the result might have been very different if everyone had behaved like Arthur and myself.

Gingold and Baddeley were and are absolute opposites. A year or two ago I did a B.B.C. television series called 'Before the Fringe'; it was a re-cap of sketches and numbers we'd done in revues years ago—long before those four brilliant young men changed intimate revue for ever overnight, just as John Osborne changed the conventional straight play overnight. Perhaps not for *ever*; I have the feeling that the pendulum is swinging back, but between them they certainly made it very difficult for many years to get produced in London either a conventional revue or what used to be called a drawing-room comedy, with French windows and stairs and, of all things, a plot. I was a little scared of 'Before the Fringe'; I thought it might be just another melancholy meander down Memory Lane. The exciting thing was that teen-agers came up and said, "I didn't know you could get away with all that dirt in those days". "Those days" I didn't much care for, but it was good to have it proved that the old stuff was still acceptable. In one of the 'Before the Fringe' shows the entire cast consisted of Gingold, Baddeley, and myself as compère and making the odd appearance (some of them very odd indeed) in sketches. Nothing had changed. We rehearsed in a depressing and dirty church hall in Paddington; when planning Television Centre, the architects thought of everything —restaurants, bars, V.I.P. suites, showers, and so on—but omitted to include any space where actors might learn their words. On the Monday morning rehearsal of the Gingold-Baddeley 'Before the Fringe' the girls ran true to form. Rehearsal was at ten a.m.; I arrived from Brighton at around a quarter to and found Gingold sitting alone, having been there for half-an-hour, and as usual word-perfect. Baddeley arrived forty-five minutes late, again with two dogs and a number of rather strange camp-followers, not knowing a word. They said, "Hullo, darling", kissed one another rather distantly and after the dogs had been taken out walkies and given their elevenses, the ladies got down to work. The results were equally satisfactory; but whereas in Gingold's case one thought, "She knows it now perfectly; by Friday when we put the show in the can she can only havē got worse, not better," in Baddeley's case one just thought "She'll *never* know it." Different methods; different approach. But both of them dear talented ladies.

There are, of course, exceptions—well, I suppose there must be—but the great majority of comediennes are kleptomaniacs. I don't mean they go around sneaking other people's salt-cellars or after-shave lotion into their handbags; but as far as material is concerned—particularly successful material —they are definitely light-fingered. We had better keep them anonymous, but one very famous comedienne was appearing once in cabaret at the Colony Club in London, using a great deal of my material without so much as a by-your-leave. Not that one bothered about the by-your-leave; it was the money I was after. I went to her first night (she thought I was safely on the other side of the Rhine); just before midnight a rather squalid green baize card-table was sneaked in on one side of the band's dais with her props and funny hats on it. "That's my number," I said to the people who were with me. "And so's that and that; I'm not sure about *that*." The card-table was whisked away and the comedienne's act swiftly re-arranged. Another of the breed, equally famous, appeared some years ago in a disastrous revue in New York. She must have known that sooner or later someone would find out but unfortunately for her, Terence Rattigan was at the first night and flew home immediately after it, bringing back the pro-gramme and ringing me up the following morning to say did I know you-know-who was doing such-and-such a number of mine—that, what was more, the programme credit was *"By* you-know-who." We slapped in an injunction saying curtain shall not rise tonight, the impresario putting on the show had a coronary and died, and the whole thing was highly embar-rassing. Comediennes are all the same; after they have been doing someone's material for any length of time, they genu-inely believe it is their property and that they wrote it. And of course any comedienne going out to, say, Australia, just packs a suitcase full of other people's scripts and flogs them as her own. One came back from an Australian tour and told me quite frankly that she found to her disgust that all the material of mine she was going to do down under had already been done down under. I said I knew, and not a penny piece had I received, which was precisely the same amount I would have got if she had done the stuff. They never do it with bacon or margarine or gin; they pay for those. But they hate paying for material. You have to employ bloodhounds or send Securicor out to the ends of piers at summer seasons to have any chance of getting any money. They are all dear, sweet girls, but, where material is concerned, definitely kleptomaniacs.

The three revues at the Ambassadors were, in a way, unique. Baddeley had moved elsewhere and Gingold was the presiding genius with, in the first show, Crisham as her co-star and, in the two others, Henry Kendall. The first of the trinity got the most fabulous press; when we decided to do a successor or second edition, everyone said, "Well, they'll never top *that*." *Sweeter and Lower* got an even better press than *Sweet and Low* and ran for 870 performances. When we elected to do a third and completely new edition, the same people said we were mad, stretching our luck really too far, and about to commit theatrical suicide; *Sweetest and Lowest* got the best press of the three and lasted for 791 wonderful days and nights. Thanks to expert direction by Charles Hickman, delightful music by Charles Zwar, exquisite costumes and décor by Berkeley Sutcliffe —and above all thanks to the company and especially to la Gingold—the three shows did me proud and completely changed my life. Even Uncle James from Berwick seemed almost inclined to say, "All is forgiven" without actually adding the words, "come back". He came to London once for some timber conference and I took him out to lunch at a very expensive restaurant and made a point of ordering the dearest wine on the wine-list. It didn't taste very nice, which served me right. It was Chateau d'Yquem, which in those days I thought was the chic thing to order; it was far too sweet and in any case we were eating steak.

You would have thought that by the third revue the critics might have run out of superlatives but they gallantly struggled to maintain the paeans. It is an obnoxious habit to quote one's own notices, especially if they are good, but James Agate paid me the greatest compliment I have ever received when, after *Sweetest and Lowest*, he wrote that I had "taken rank with the great masters of revue—Ronald Jeans, Herbert Farjeon, Noël Coward". I don't keep notices (I stopped keeping them after the first night of *Jonathan*), but I kept that one and still have it. Ronald Jeans and Farjeon I had always revered; the Master I still do. Mr. Agate went on to say, "I venture to suggest that on the strength of his latest performance, Meilhac and Halevy would have hailed Mr. Melville as kindred spirit and brother artist." I was still pretty dumb and had to look up Meilhac and Halevy to find out who they were; they turned out to be Offenbach's librettists, so I suppose that was all right.

The audiences at the Ambassadors throughout those five years were not so much audiences as a loyal and faithful congregation; more correctly, members of a club. They boasted to each other how many times they'd seen the show and the tiny dress-circle bar was packed with fully paid-up members, most of them on leave in London slapping one another on the back, nipping in to stand at the side of the dress-circle to catch their favourite sketch or number, and then nipping out again to finish their round of gins and order another. America was now well and truly in the war (I cannot believe through any influence on the part of 'Front Line Family') and the Americans fell hook, line and sinker for Gingold. And vice versa. It was impossible to get near her dressing-room for the queue. Some of our transatlantic cousins got a little confused about her; they had never seen anything quite like her before. A strapping U.S. Marine was overheard recommending the show to a buddy in a London pub; "You wanna catch this show at the Ambassadors," he said. "It's got this guy Hormone Gielgud in it; he does the whole show in drag and, boy, is he a knock-out." The Americans, in fact, fell so strongly for Ging that in the third edition we put in a number to cement even further this cordial transatlantic relationship. Henry Kendall rather stole the tag of the number by appearing as the Statue of Liberty, but for the Yanks in the audience it was Gingold's knock-out blow. After a highly dramatic verse about Christopher Columbus sailing west to discover the New World (which, of course, he didn't) and now thousands of brave boys pouring east in convoy to save the ancient civilisation from which Chris had sailed, the number went into rhythm and Miss G., slapping her shapely thighs like the sort of pantomime principal boy we used to get before Jess Conrad and Mark Wynter muscled in on the racket, brought the house down nightly with the immortal words:

> Thanks, Yanks! . . .
> For all that you've done;
> For bringing us fun
> As well as those guns and those tanks—
> The least we can say is 'thanks'.
> Thanks, Yanks! . . .
> That very nice boy
> From old Illinois
> Who led an attack on my flanks—
> The least I could say was 'thanks'.
> > Co-operation
> > And less isolation
> > Is surely a swell recipe;
> > I murmur 'thank 'ee'
> > To each charming Yankee
> > For all that they've done—to me.
> So thanks, Yanks! . . .
> For creating a boom
> In my dressing-room—
> So far I've not drawn any blanks—
> And the least one can say is *'thanks'*.

The only time Miss Gingold failed to bring the house down was occasionally on a Thursday matinée when we sometimes got audiences who didn't quite understand all that we were getting at and made disapproving clucking teeth noises on lines like "led an attack on my flanks". One Thursday towards the end of the run I went into the foyer just as the matinée audience was coming out; business seemed to be if anything healthier than usual and it transpired that the Women's Rural Institute from, I think, High Wycombe, was having its annual outing in London and had decided that the revue should be part of the revels. It was again pouring with rain and when I arrived at the theatre the foyer was jammed with W.R.I., peeling on plastic macks and pixie-hoods. A more disgruntled collection of femininity it would be difficult to imagine; they had obviously detested every second of the show and if *The Sound of Music* had been on at the time would clearly have preferred that. After several minutes of grizzling, the unfortunate woman who had organised the outing rounded on the malcontents and shouted, right in my ear, "Oh, for heaven's sake, *shut up*. We've made a mistake, let's face it; now let's have our tea."

The Ambassadors in those days was run by an elderly charmer called Jack Pemberton, who was not so much interested (except financially) in the show as a whole, as in the most amenable girl in the chorus. He had a partner called Harry Dubens who was a lovable Jew who had trouble with his v's and w's. Once, when we were having one of our habitual crises and shouting-matches (I forget who the target was on this occasion, but I had obviously taken a turn against someone) he took my arm and walked me round the block which separated, if only just, the Ambassadors from the Ivy Restaurant and told me "Not to vorry, my dear. The man has no wehemence, no wirulance, and vot is vorse, no *vit*."

On the second of the two last performances of the final show in the threesome (we had to have two because of the demand for seats) the gallery faithfuls, led by an outsize fanatic called Sophie, began queueing forty-eight hours before the curtain went up. Gingold and I took them out tea and hot soup, feeling rather like Lady Bountiful dispensing largesse to the peasantry. When at last the curtain came down at around one in the morning, Gingold clutched me centre-stage and with the tears flooding and her mascara cascading down her cheeks, said, "They say you'll never write for me again." "I know, darling," I said, also with the tears flowing and both my after-shave and perspiration running down my cheeks. "And it's *true*." Apart from a one-minute sketch in that television show when the two Hermiones were briefly re-united, I never have. As the Pickwick character said, "Anythin' for a quiet life, as the man said ven he took the sitivation at the lighthouse."

4

THE FLAT I had leased in Grape Street was L-shaped and the
L went round the corner where the top of Shaftesbury Avenue
meets New Oxford Street. It must without doubt have been
the noisiest flat in London; everyone changed gears, tooted,
or jammed on their brakes at the traffic lights at that corner.
No visitor to the flat slept a wink; I never heard a sound.
When I moved to a deathly quiet terrace house in Brighton,
it took me several months to get used to the stillness; I was
wakened every morning long before dawn by the deafening
din of birds. As well as the noise, the flat had one other distinction—what must have been equally without doubt the
oldest lift in London. You had first to close two very insecure
metal doors which badly needed oiling and behaved like
complaining concertinas; once in the death-trap you gave a
fierce yank to a frayed rope and the lift set out on its journey,
rocking from one side of the shaft to the other and making
even more noise than the traffic outside. Things were comparatively simple going down to the ground floor of the
block; the lift just crash-landed on the concrete base at the
bottom of the shaft and after a few shudders and shakes stayed
there, wheezing. Going up to the top floor of the building
was more dangerous; unless you were very careful in yank-
ing, the cage ricochetted off the roof and went hurtling down
again to the basement. And attempting to stop the thing at
any intermediary floor was lethal. You had to grasp the rope
at the correct distance from the floor you hoped to stop at and

yank in the opposite direction to the one you were travelling in; unless you wore gloves, and heavy gloves at that, this drew blood.

It might not have been necessary to reveal these graphic details of the Grape Street lift's oddities were it not for the fact that James Agate lived in the flat immediately below mine. It was Mr. Agate's wont to go off to the theatre and after writing his piece, usually managing to include apt quotations from Voltaire or de la Rochefoucauld even in his review of an Ivor Novello musical, repair either to the Savage Club or the Café Royal for refreshment. The Café Royal was no longer the Bohemian rendezvous it had been before or even after World War I, but in Agate's presence it almost became so. Jimmy could have made a transport café on the A23 seem gay; he probably did. He teetered back to Grape Street usually around two or three in the morning and after slight front door trouble began his losing battle with the lift. I would lie in bed and listen first to the clanging of the lift doors, outer and inner, and then to the noise of the cage rocketing upwards, past Mr. Agate's flat, past mine, past the flat above me and on and up until it hit the roof of the building with an almighty crash, rebounded off it, and started thundering unsteadily down to the basement. Often this went on for anything up to a quarter of an hour, punctuated by fearsome oaths from the distinguished dramatic critic of the *Sunday Times*. I would think, "Rot him; why should I leave a nice warm bed to rescue the old boy?" Prudence and self-interest always, however, prevailed; after all, I might well need another notice like the one he had given me for *Sweetest and Lowest* and it would not have looked good if it became known that I had left him to starve to death yo-yo-ing up and down all night in the original lift that Miss Waygood-Otis regretted. Night after night, or rather morning after morning, I got up, put on a dressing-gown and bedroom slippers, and went out on the landing to effect the rescue

86

operation. This was the most hazardous task of all; you had to insert one hand through the diamond-shaped pattern of the lift's inner door, grab the rope and yank. Mr. Agate, when freed, was always profoundly grateful and unless he was expecting a visitor usually invited me in to his flat for a Scotch and an extremely interesting if lengthy, dissertation on the past and present policy of the Comédie Française. If this hadn't happened at three a.m., I am sure I would have been fascinated. All I really wanted was to get back to bed.

The first time I did the Grace Darling act and got Mr. Agate out of the lift and was invited in to his flat, there was in his study a more than life-size portrait of an extremely handsome young man wearing a black rubber mackintosh; it gave me a bit of a turn. There were also in prominent positions on Mr. Agate's desk, three canes; and, particularly as I was wearing only pyjamas and a dressing-gown, I assumed the worst. Mr. Agate held up one of the canes, fixed me with what I took for a sadistic leer, and said, "Now, young man : you think you're going to make a career in the theatre. Tell me : whose cane was this?" I said, "It could, sir, have been George Robey's." "It not only could," said Mr. Agate. "It was." Picking up the second cane, he said, "And this?" Gulping, I said, "Er, Chaplin's ...?" "Correct," said Mr. Agate, and picked up the third cane which was a more sophisticated example with a silver top. I said, "Well, it might be Fred Astaire, but I *think* it's Hetty King." "You'll do," said Mr. Agate. "Sit down; have a drink. You are, of course, too young ever to have seen the divine Sarah, but I remember ..." And we were off.

Agate was a wonderful character and the sort of man I think a critic ought to be, and today rarely is. He genuinely loved the theatre; he went off to each first night sincerely hoping that the show would be good and that he could be read next morning raving about it. It seems to me that nowadays —at any rate to judge by their faces on arriving at a theatre and certainly when getting together in the bar at the interval, many present-day dramatic critics come to the theatre praying for disaster. One cannot really blame them; today bad news is more newsworthy than good news. But Agate was not just a highly perceptive critic, he was an enthusiast and a most readable writer. I have all his 'Egos' and various collections of his criticisms on the shelves in my bedroom; I can take down one of the books and re-read for the umpteenth time a notice he wrote of some play that opened in London thirty or more years ago, and it brings that play alive. I saw the first night of Robert Helpmann's *Hamlet*, produced jointly by Tyrone Guthrie and Michael Benthall at the New in 1944; re-reading Agate's notice of it brings every detail of the production back; and what an eye for detail the man had . . .

On reflection I must hold that Messrs. Guthrie and Benthall's production beat Mr. Helpmann's Hamlet not by a head but by half a dozen lengths. The fashionable, one-set affair, of course. On the left, an exiguous battlement. In the centre a huge column of the kind against which the German painter Winterhalter used to pose the young Queen Victoria. On the right a potting-shed to serve as powder-closet for Gertrude and sepulchre for Ophelia. Up-stage a sloping runway making the whole thing look like a combination of the old Café Royal and the approach to Liverpool Street Station. The lighting? Total black-out with stabbings of jay-walkers' torches held at impermissible angles. As usual with these ultra-highbrow jamborees the most elementary mistakes were made. The Ghost's voice came clearly from back-stage instead of the cellar. In the play scene one saw little of the mimic drama, which was done sideways. The King? He was so be-thronged by that producer's toy, a crowd, that one forgot to note him, despite Mr. Basil Sydney's previous excellences. The Queen, neglecting to watch the show, half turned her back on it and challenged the audience with her handsome brow and un-winking Cyclopean jewel. Don't tell me that a first night at Elsinore was so common an occurrence that Gertrude was bored; she was not a dramatic critic. Hamlet? He peered over shoulders, peeped under arms, and dodged about in the manner of Dopey in *Snow White*. Yet Mr. Helpmann had begun very well. Sitting apart, his head against a piece of Windsor Castle, he was a most heart-taking little figure. And how like Sarah! The same tousled mop, the same profile, the same collarette, the same provocation, the same elegance. I found myself murmuring with Phèdre : Il avait votre port, vos yeux, votre langage.

And yet, just as no-one ever accused Sarah of masculin-ity, so Helpmann nowhere suggested the feminine; this was acting on the adrogynous plane of pure poetry, as indeed one expected from an artist in the school of Nijinsky. But poetry, which includes poise and pose and gait and gesture, is not enough for Shakespeare's undanced crea-tion. The essence of Hamlet is an ingrained melancholy, of which Mr. Helpmann gave no sign. The virtuoso pas-sages were well brought off because Mr. Helpmann is a born actor and a virtuoso. But the basis of this impersona-tion was gaminerie, Eulenspiegel rather than Hamlet. Enchanting if you like, but the wrong kind of enchant-ment. The trouble with this production is that Mr. Helpmann is not a great actor, but a charming one who reduces Hamlet to the size of the figures in a canvas by James Pryde. Will they never realise that a great actor's punch is more potent than a hog's-head of team spirit?

Does any present-day dramatic critic write with that kind of perception or with that *knowledge*? I doubt it. He has everything right; it is as though the set had been photographed and one was looking at the photograph twenty-six years later. Gertrude's closet and/or Ophelia's selpulchre *was* a potting-shed; the centre runway *did* look like a combination of the old Café Royal and the approach to Liverpool Street Station. The voice of the Ghost *did* come from quite the wrong place. And Margot Grahame, as the Queen, obviously *was* bored stiff in the play scene. This is, in my view, valuable constructive criticism; Agate's notices almost always were. After reading such reviews things can be put right by those concerned; in this particular instance, the voice of the Ghost came from a more believable direction on the second night of the run. The Phèdre quotation is, of course, dragged in by *la poignée de son cou* (the scruff of its neck), but you expected that from Agate. And many even of the *Sunday Times'* more erudite readers would have had to look up "adrogynous"; that, too, was typical. I can see him chortling when he wrote the word and saying, "That'll send the ignorant bastards scuttling to their dictionaries." Incidentally, the night after Helpmann's *Hamlet* opened at the New only a few hundreds yards from the Ambassadors, a new number was inserted into *Sweetest and Lowest* with Gingold as a rival and even less melancholy Dane. She began with a line which was not mine—"speak the speech, I pray you, trippingly on the tongue"—and proceeded:

> And, goodness, how rippingly
> And indeed trippingly
> *Hamlet*'s been done at the New.
> With gay entrechats
> And the talk of the bars
> Is how Bobby looks—well, twenty-two . . .
>   (from the back of the dress circle).

She then warmed to her subject. Even in the forties, intimate revue may have been parochial, but it was nothing if not topical.

The lady in the flat above mine in Grape Street was another splendid Scottish character actress called Elliot Mason; we were a very theatrical block. Miss Mason had been one of the stalwarts of the Scottish National Players in the days when I was sent starry-eyed by them in the King's Theatre, Greenock; she was now well established in the West End, and in with H.M. Tennent and Emlyn Williams and all who mattered. She was a dear, and I only saw her once rattled. She was appearing in a play called *The Young Mrs. Barrington* at the Winter Garden just down the road from the flats; it was a big success and had a long run. After one performance, Miss Mason was waylaid by a fan on coming out of the stage door and graciously agreed that the fan—an earnest lady in brogues—should accompany her back to Grape Street but no further. Until they parted company on the doorstep it was a harmonious trek. "You've given me so much pleasure," the fan kept repeating. "I've seen everything you've ever done: theatre, films, everything. I can honestly say there's no-one else who's brought me such genuine delight." "Well, thank you very much," said Miss Mason, purring while fumbling for her key at the entrance to No. 3, Grape Street. "No," the fan insisted. "It's *me* that's got to thank *you*, Miss Rutherford." Miss Mason came straight up to my flat and exploded. "Margaret Rutherford, of all people," she said. "If I weren't a strict teetotaller, I'd be at that bottle of gin over there in a flash."

The reason I was able to live comfortably in the flat (or as comfortably as one could in the blitz) was that I had been posted yet again—I must have cost the R.A.F. a fortune in stamps—this time to a somewhat bizarre affair called Air Information. This was a joint Anglo-American set-up, organised—if one can use the word without blushing—to handle the press and sound radio coverage of the liberation of Europe if and when this happened. I was in the sound radio department on the R.A.F. side; my opposite number in the

U.S.A.A.F. was Ben Lyon. My boss was Lord Willoughby de Broke, whom I see every now and then at race meetings and think how much happier he is looking than in the days when he was in charge of long and argumentative sessions in his office at Air Ministry involving the press, R.A.F. and U.S.A.A.F. serving personnel, and permanent civil servants whose creed was to keep everything a deathly secret. It was obvious that sooner or later the Allies would have to invade Europe; the Germans had unaccountably omitted to invade Britain (except for landing on the Channel Islands where, at any rate on Sark, they were put firmly in their place by the Dame of that enchanting island and told to get down to work, mainly on the Dame's garden and her courtyard, which needed re-paving); Hitler had amazingly struck instead at Russia and Stalin kept dropping rather pointed hints that a little diversion in Europe might help. Air Inf., accordingly, was put into top gear to ensure that when this happened everyone would know all about it, in spite of the permanent civil servants. A great many things had to be planned, all in absolute secrecy, which oddly enough is easier when dealing with Fleet Street than in many other walks of life; journalists exist on stories just as actors exist on applause, but tell them something is Top Secret or off the record and the vast majority respect the ruling. Conducting officers had to be found and trained to steer the war correspondents roughly to the right places at roughly the right times, briefing officers geared to tell the journalists in advance what was going to happen (without going into too great detail in case it didn't) or explain away what had happened (without, again, confessing that things had gone monumentally awry); jeeps and equipment and accommodation for an army of press-men, photographers, feature writers, sound radio commentators and the lot, both British and American; all this and much more had to be laid on. When the plans were more or less finalised, it was discovered that there was no-one to cover on sound radio the British air side of the actual invasion and subsequent events; in other words the task which our Tactical Air Force had to carry out. Which was not unimportant. The B.B.C. had allotted their maximum of war correspondents to the invasion; Frank Gillard to the army; Stanley Maxted (a dear man) mainly to the coverage of such subsequent disasters as the drop on Arnhem; Stewart Macpherson concentrating mostly on .Canadian participation; Wynford Vaughan Thomas doing excitable reports on the whole scene right up to the time he found himself broadcasting from Hitler's desk in the Chancellery on the day Berlin fell—which, for once, though I am sure he was delighted to be sitting in Hitler's chair at long last, seemed to have a sobering effect on Wynford's natural Welsh ebullience; these and many others. But there was no-one available to handle the Tactical Air Force coverage of the invasion when it came. Muggins, of course, said he would do it. The B.B.C. were delighted; they were getting an additional war correspondent at no extra cost; the Air Ministry were quite happy about the arrangement, not having worked out that anyone pretending to be a war correspondent while still wearing R.A.F. uniform was bound to run into trouble. But I think Air Ministry had begun, understandably, to get a little tired of me and were happy to see my rear view. We had three chief P.R.O.'s at the head-quarters of Bomber, Fighter and Coastal Commands; until muggins said he would invade, it had been muggins' job to get the Bomber, Fighter, or Coastal Command pilots or navigators or rear-gunners up to London to meet the press or record for the B.B.C. whenever they had a story. Coastal Command was always co-operative; Bomber Command held sternly to the view that publicity should be confined to the official communiqué saying that x hundred tons of high explosives had been dropped on the china of Dresden or that y aircraft had failed to return; and the Fighter Command P.R.O. just said cheerfully on the phone, "Sorry, old boy;

93

the ones that got back went out and got pissed and they're still sleeping it off." I saw the Fighter Command point of view, but I used to grizzle about the whole situation at our morning meetings at Air Ministry and I am sure they were all relieved when muggins volunteered to play a very minor walk-on part in the invasion drama.

In the early spring of 1944 we were all hermetically sealed in a camp near Hambledon in Hampshire, where cricket was invented. This was the start of—to me—a series of astonishments; there were a great many of us and as the weeks went by leading up to the invasion—quite apart from ourselves—the most colossal concentration of armour and vehicles built up. Tanks, armoured cars, guns, jeeps, wagons, trailers and the lot were piled cheek-by-jowl or bumper-to-bumper along the Hampshire hedgerows; there were some rather amateurish attempts to camouflage them with branches of trees or bundles of hay, but you would have thought that *someone* on the opposition (or even some friend of theirs over here) would have noticed that something was afoot. At sea, an armada of over four thousand ships was slowly but deliberately concentrating on Portsmouth, Southampton, the Isle of Wight and other South Coast resorts. And nothing happened; the enemy, admittedly by then somewhat concerned by the way things were going in Russia, continued to bomb London and Coventry and other cities but apparently failed to notice that anything untoward was going on down on the South Coast.

We were superbly briefed. All sorts of officers, culminating with Montgomery, came down to the camp and told us precisely what was going to happen, how, with what, and where. Not when. And not really where; the maps we were shown of the various sectors of the invasion area had no names of towns or villages on them, or if they had, the names were false. I had brought into the camp (we were under canvas, and in the later stages of the briefing period not even allowed into the nearest village in case we blabbed) an old edition of that admirable publication, the *Guide Michelin*. I had a feeling in my water that we were going to do the obvious and go straight across; Normandy probably, perhaps further north in the Pas-de-Calais region. But I didn't think there were going to be any surprises like landing on the Cherbourg peninsula or attempting another Dieppe. At the final briefings, the coast-line where we were to land, each little indentation along the shore, the villages and hamlets a mile or so inland, were all shown to us enormously blown-up on the screen; even clock towers where snipers might be expected (and usually obliged by turning up) or clumps of trees were clearly marked. I felt I knew every inch of the ground like the back of my hand; better, perhaps. I don't know the back of my hand very intimately, the nicotine stains worry me and I try not to look. On the extreme left flank of the sector where our little lot were to land—in whatever country, it might still have been Norway, and the Germans, bless them, obviously had decided it was going to be—there was a dip in the contour of the coast-line just before what was obviously the entrance to a little port or harbour. I went back to my tent and was prepared to comb through *Michelin* from Abbeville to Yvetot, in the hope of finding out exactly where that little harbour was. In addition to the guide's excellent service in advising you that the best place to stay at in Sully-sur-Loire is Madame Burgerin's Hotel de la Poste and the best thing to eat while staying there is her gratin de ris de veau Sullyloise, the guide contains highly accurate little street maps of any sizeable town in France. I went laboriously through it until about halfway when I found exactly the coast-line contour and the shape of the entrance to the harbour which we had been shown in the briefing. It was a nasty little town in Normandy called Ouistreham; and the moment I knew where we were going to land—a few hundred kilometres to the right of that entrance to the harbour of Ouistreham—I wished I didn't know. I thought: my God, one night I'll give it away, probably to someone who is either a spy or checking up on security. I was given leave to go to London to do a special job; I was terrified in case I got plastered and let out not only the fact that the invasion was imminent but also where my little section of it was to land. I went to the show at the Ambassadors and had supper afterwards with some of the cast; they kept asking, "What's *happening*, dear?" and I kept replying, "Nothing, really; it's all very dull." When Harry Kendall said he must go and have a wee-wee, I started thinking of Ouistreham and went, for me, quite pale.

The special job was to record for the B.B.C. and other networks the eve-of-invasion messages to the forces by Eisenhower and Tedder. They were a fascinating contrast. I went into Ike's office at his headquarters; the microphone had already been fitted up on his desk and the engineers were at the ready in the recording van parked outside. Ike came in, sat at his desk, said, "Okay?" and reeled off his piece. When, a few moments after he had finished, we got the clearance from the van outside, he said, "Sure it was okay? Thanks a lot." And left. I then crossed the corridor to Tedder's office; he was waiting there rather nervously. "I don't think I'm very good at this sort of thing," he said. I made encouraging noises as befitted my station; I was a Pilot Officer at the time, never having piloted so much as a kiddie-car since the outbreak of war; he, after all, was an Air Marshal. He recorded his message and he was dead right; he wasn't very good at that sort of thing. A great many ums and ers, and a rather wavering high-pitched voice. When it was over and I'd said, "Thank you very much, sir; absolutely splendid," he said, "I couldn't by any possible chance hear it, could I?" This was the last thing I wanted but it is difficult for a Pilot Officer to say, "No, you can't" to an Air Marshal. He heard the play-back and was rightly appalled. "But I don't speak like *that*," he said. Again it is difficult for a Pilot Officer to say to an Air Marshal, "You do, you know, chum." We recorded the piece with Tedder doing his best to lower his voice and cut out the ums and ers; the whole thing took about two hours as against Eisenhower's five minutes. Not that it mattered; recording engineers can accomplish miracles and most of the ums and ers were removed and the voice taken down by about half an octave. I once recorded a talk by Dame Megan Lloyd George, who had an odd habit of audibly taking in a breath between phrases, a habit which she hotly denied even when hearing herself on the play-back. "I don't make those wheezing noises," she said. "It just isn't *true*. There must be something wrong with your machine." The engineer who was editing the recording cut all the intakes of breath from the tape and we gave them to Dame Megan in an envelope as a souvenir. She was quite grateful but still distrustful about the whole thing.

The next miracle, and to me the greatest of all, was that the enemy failed to notice that the invasion was on. I detest using the word "enemy", especially after this long lapse of time. Some of my greatest friends are German; I stay in Munich with Erik Charell, the producer of *White Horse Inn* and many other huge successes, and he gives me more kindness and hospitality than almost anyone else I have ever known; the son of good friends of mine in Hamburg stays with me in Brighton every year and calls me "Nunkel" and makes me laugh and feel young. Or younger. I find it difficult to believe that these are the people we had to fight, and fight twice. But, though individually so charming, as a nation misled they are dangerous. Charell once told me, when I seemed mystified why Hitler had started the trouble in, of all places, Munich, and I had found the beer-kellers packed with the most delightful, well-behaved and intelligent students: "You must understand, my dear. Hitler chose München for a very good reason. When you drink beer in Bavaria, after two beers you are good friends; after three, you begin singing; after four, Bavaria is a better place than any other part of Germany; after six, Germany is the greatest country in the world and you get up on the tables and the knives come out."

In the spring of 1944, the few Germans who were on leave or stationed in or around Munich must, I suppose, have been at or on or under those tables in the beer-kellers, no doubt listening to the radio, gloating over the helpless state of the poor British, worried about the Russian situation, singing the Hörst Wessel song and ordering steins again all round. For once, German efficiency failed. The armada sailed, a day late because of a last-minute weather change; you would have thought someone might even have noticed *that*. The four thousand or more ships slipped anchor on the night of June 5th/6th, 1944, and crossed a Channel which had barely a ripple in it. It was a clear moonlight night; not an enemy aircraft came near us until we were almost off the Normandy coast and very few even then. I know that fiendishly clever things were being done on radar to give the impression that a major air drop was taking place in Norway; I know, too, that the German armour had been deployed to anticipate a landing anywhere else than in Normandy (it was very smartly moved back to the right positions); but it still seems astounding to me that not a single German reconnaissance plane came out that night, looked down on the Channel, and signalled back to base, "I don't want to sound in any way an alarmist, but I *think* something's happening."

I had a jeep containing my recording gear, a bottle of Scotch, for some strange reason a box of shortbread which Nell Ballantyne had given me, and an R.A.F. photographer called Alf who seemed worried about the whole thing. I had also to begin with had a driver. His name was Mike; he was a splendid character, and a born scrounger. He was all for the comforts of life; as soon as he joined me in the camp at

Hambledon, he decided that it would be cosier to sleep in the back of one of the lorries than under canvas like the rest of the hoi-polloi. He requisitioned a number of mattresses, Lilo's, blankets, pillows and even an eiderdown, and slept the sleep of the just in the back of his lorry until the night he omitted to put up the rear flap. At two in the morning he turned over, fell out of the lorry, dislocated his shoulder and fractured an elbow, and remained on the ground and out for the count until I found him early next morning. He had to be packed off to hospital, and as his interrupted slumber happened only three nights before D-day and there was no possibility of getting a replacement, there was nothing for it but to drive the jeep myself.

I also took with me four pigeons. The R.A.F. had decided that in case all other means of communication failed, pigeons were the thing. There was even a Wing-Commander (P), the (P) in brackets after his name standing for pigeons. For several months before D-day, he organised tremendously serious trial exercises with the pigeons and pigeon-fanciers, if they were fanciers, serving under him. Birds and erks would be sent up to the North of Scotland, the erks would write out dummy messages on a sort of rice paper and clip these on the birds' legs, and the birds would be released with the idea that they would tear back at a rate of knots to their roosting-place down South. Most of them, to be fair, did; but there was usually one bird more intelligent than the others who worked the whole thing out, saw a nice tree or telegraph-wire in, say, Leicestershire or Rutland, and just said to itself, "Nuts, let's doss down here." As the messages on the rice paper had been written consecutively and formed part of one complete signal, the missing section attached to the leg of the more intelligent bird rendered the whole thing incomprehensible. However, the Wing-Commander (P) was never daunted. He brought a selection of pigeons to the camp at Hambledon, and enthusiastically instructed me how to handle them, feed them, get on the right side of them, attach the messages to their ridiculous little legs without actually breaking them, and release the beastly things. At exactly the right time before we left camp to embark on the invasion, the four birds who had been specially chosen for the journey were delivered to me in a wicker cage, complete with their rations and a set of neat little white plastic trays for their drinkies. I was given the most detailed instructions about feeding times, drinking hours, and how to keep them calm and unflurried in the event of enemy action on the way across. Apparently the foursome had been brought to such a pitch of preparation (it is, I suppose, like a bitch being on heat) that the delay of the invasion by even one day completely ruined the whole arrangement; I received a signal from the Wing-Commander (P) telling me to release them. This I did gladly, thankful to see the backs of all four, and attaching rather ribald messages to their legs. I was delighted; four pigeons, plus their foodstuff and drinking dishes, are not the sort of encumbrance one really wants to be lumbered with when liberating Europe. To my horror, when we were lying off the Isle of Wight waiting to come under starter's orders, a very smart R.A.F. motor-launch swished alongside our landing-craft and four substitute birds were hoisted on deck. The naval personnel running the L.S.T. thought it was about the funniest thing that had ever happened; there were a great many witticisms about birds being just what they needed at that moment. The new quartette were christened Blood, Sweat, Toil and Tears; Blood was released halfway across the Channel with a stirring message saying we were halfway across the Channel; it occurred to me that if the bird flew in the wrong direction it would give the whole thing away, but fortunately it didn't. It went pelting back to Angleterre. Sweat (who had taken a turn against me, it was mutual) gave one of my fingers a vicious peck when I was filling its drinking tray with fresh water; it was the only time I lost blood in the entire campaign, and the bird was dispatched at once without any message at all tethered to its limb in the hope that he/she/it would be in disgrace for having lost his, her or its little bit of rice paper before homing. Toil and Tears were both released as soon as we landed on the beaches, both with rather hysterical reports saying that we *had* landed, as if by then everyone didn't know. They circled over the sand dunes once or twice and then belted for home; considering all that was going on at the time I didn't blame them and indeed would have been glad to have joined them. One of the two—Toil, I think, it seemed to me the more astute of the pair—packed in the whole thing somewhere en route and was never seen or heard of again; but the other bird made the evening papers and was subsequently given the animals' V.C. or some such meritorious award for gallantry under enemy fire.

On its way to embark, the convoy was halted on the Portsmouth road and the photographer and I went into a little tobacconist and sweet-shop to stock up with Mars bars and other essentials for an invasion. I remember being very peeved indeed when the lady behind the counter took our money; she was obviously doing a roaring trade and I felt it unfair of her to charge when her customers were setting out to save her from Nazi tyranny. She even tried to short-change me, but her attention was drawn to that very swiftly. When I drove the jeep (in reverse, for some reason, I cannot remember why) up the ramp on to the landing-craft—L.S.T. 302, it was—we ran into a certain amount of trouble and were greeted with ironical cheers and some moderately obscene observations from the troops already on board; the four pigeons strapped in their wicker basket to the back of the vehicle didn't help. After some time and with a mounting smell of burning rubber I found I had left the brake on.

It was generally supposed that Monday, June 5th, was to be der Tag. The German radio had announced the fact with a good deal of embroidery concerning their readiness for the event. But on that Sunday afternoon a stiff westerly breeze blew up, there was a lot of cloud and some rain, and conditions—after weeks of the most glorious weather—could not have been worse. D-day was postponed for at least twenty-four hours. On the Monday afternoon I wandered into the ward-room and found it looking like a bargain basement during the Christmas sales. The Officer Commanding all the troops on board was briefing the officers of each unit and issuing their maps. I hadn't been told of this performance, but it was quite usual for the Army to forget that there was an R.A.F. detachment (however small and however peculiar) among them. Anyway, I joined the mêlée and found that the trip was definitely on: D-day, June 6th: H-hour, so far as we were concerned, 0720. And *Michelin* and I were right: we were to land on the beach just west of Ouistreham, on the mouth of the River Orne; our sector extended west to around the village of Luc-sur-mer, where we were to be flanked by the Canadians. Our first main objective was the town of Caen, which on our bogus maps at the briefing had been marked as "Poland". Everyone was issued with voluminous packages of real maps, except me. The Army disclaimed all responsibility for this and said they assumed the R.A.F. were making their own arrangements. Maybe they were; but it would have been nice to know to what vessel of the invasion fleet my maps had been delivered. As it was, I went to France armed with a 1939 *Michelin* guide and no driver; as a final straw I found that I had been supplied with .45 ammunition for a .38 revolver. After the briefing, I again looked up Ouistreham in the *Michelin*; it was interesting to note that the casino opened for the season on June 10th, and that the specialité de la maison at the leading restaurant was soufflé au Grand-Marnier.

We weighed anchor just after half-past six. The mine-sweepers went ahead of us and cleared narrow lanes in the minefields right up to the beaches. Everything happened exactly as it had been set down on paper. At nine o'clock the captain of the L.S.T. asked me to read the bon voyage messages from Admiral Ramsay, Admiral Talbot and General Eisenhower over the ship's public-address system. They seemed unreal, out of touch with our own little situation. The one padre on board held a short service, standing on an upturned packing-case in front of the galley door. We sang the pops 'Abide With Me' and 'O God our Help in Ages Past'; the ratings manning the gun turret above us joined in the singing, but never stopped scanning the sky. At eleven precisely, when we were due to find the battleships of the Royal Navy on our port bow, there they were ... Ramillies, Warspite, Frobisher, Mauritius, Dragon, Arethusa. It never really got dark that night; you were always able to make out grey shadows and have a guess at what type of craft they were. It was one of the quietest nights I have ever known; the last quiet night I was to enjoy for many weeks. Midway across the Channel I went back up on deck; a very young Commando was on his knees praying. When he got up, he tucked a Bible away in his battle-dress, looked round guiltily, hoping he hadn't been seen, and went below. I had my recording gear with me on deck; there was nothing to record. The greatest invasion armada of all time was crossing the Channel to smash an entrance into Europe; and it was if anything more uneventful than when I do it today and feel like a weekend in Dieppe, leave the car at Newhaven and go aboard the *Villandry* or the *Valençay*, clock in at the Aguado Hotel on the Boulevard Verdun, have moules marinières in the Moderne facing the harbour or go to the Priare in the little hamlet of Beuilly-le-bec and have the most extraordinary first course of six remarkable courses—the recipe for which Madame, who is Dame Edith Evans' double, flatly refuses to reveal—and in the evening go to the casino and lose money backing vingt-six et carré and zero. On the night of June 5th/6th, 1944, the crossing was calm, unruffled, and uninterrupted. Ahead of us, leading our own convoy, was the destroyer *Campbell*. She had played a leading part in the sinking of the *Prinz Eugen*, and had a proud veteran look about her. Guarding us to port and starboard was the rest of our escort; I must say they looked woefully inadequate. They were two scruffy little trawlers, the *Northern Gem* and the *Northern Light* . . . the sort of little ships who must have sailed from Fraserburgh or Lossiemouth in the days when I was with the B.B.C. in Aberdeen. They wore their grey war-paint and were armed against any sneaking E-boat. And nothing came near us : not an aircraft, not an E- or a U-boat. Straight ahead, towards morning, there were a few brilliant flashes from the French coast; perhaps our paratroops had already landed and were causing trouble. By H minus 2 it was light enough to see the flags on the buoys which marked our narrow lane through the mines. The skipper of the L.S.T. informed me that he was "chukker," which is the naval equivalent of being browned off, and what about going below and having a mug of cocoa. And this was what ended the war in Europe. The end took some time in coming; but this almost eerie placid trip across the Channel was the start of it.

By the time we got near the French coast it was light enough to see that at least one church tower shown to us in the briefings was no longer there. Before our arrival, of course, the paratroops had been dropped and there had been what was referred to laconically in those days as the softening-up process; something which, I feel, can never have seemed very soft to those on the receiving end. The opposition had cottoned on to the fact, if a little belatedly, that something was afoot; there was quite heavy shelling from a mile or two inland. The jeep, the photographer, the pigeons and I were comparative late-comers; we were off the beaches by around five in the morning, but I don't think we actually landed until almost a couple of hours later, by which time a great deal was happening. But we were still on what was known as the first tide; I have always been secretly proud of the fact, though to be honest those who followed us in on later tides—because of the speedy build-up of the enemy armour—had in many cases a rougher reception. The Germans may have mistakenly sent most of their Panzer divisions elsewhere; they still seemed to have quite a lot of guns and ammunition in the area. Part of the 125th Panzer Group as well as their 346th Infantry Division were in and around Ouistreham. The main body of the 125th Panzers and the 12th S.S. Brigade (the only Germans whom we grew to hate) were ringed in front of Caen. The shelling from the shore was answered enthusiastically by the Royal Navy offshore; as both sides seemed to be dropping their stuff somewhat short, being between the two was uncomfortable. The landing-craft we were on had towed behind it across the Channel what was known as a rhino, really a raft with a sort of outboard motor attached. When we got into water too shallow for the L.S.T. itself to proceed any further, the rhino was brought round to the bow of the ship and the jeeps and armoured cars manoeuvred gingerly on to it, the idea being that you then cruised gently on to the beach, said "nous voici!" and went to the nearest *estaminet* and ordered a large Calvados. It did not in fact work out that way. Muggins, it goes without saying, had managed through a miscalculation to get the jeep, the photographer, the recording gear and the two remaining pigeons for'ard (if that is the expression) and we were obviously destined to be first off. It was again like taking one's car over to Dieppe, only in reverse; when you calculate that by hanging on to the bitter end of the queue in Newhaven you will be first off in Dieppe, by some cunning means the whole thing gets switched around in mid-Channel and you find that by being last on you are also last off. You can't win. On this particular cross-Channel excursion, there we were, dead centre of the front row of the chorus with our own and the opposition's shells plopping into the sea all round us. To make matters worse, halfway on in the rhino's journey to the beach it stuck hard and fast on a sand-bank which had been overlooked by the Ordnance surveyors or maritime experts who had supposedly cased the joint. I said to the photographer (who was by now very worried indeed) "I'm not staying here, chum," revved up, put the jeep in bottom gear, and plunged off the front of the rhino. The water was much deeper than I had expected; the photographer and I were up to our necks and the pigeons were in a terrible state. All the vehicles had, of course, been waterproofed; we had been through very boring, damp tests to ensure that when we landed in water we could still make it even though submerged. Driving through even four or five feet of water is an unnerving experience; for one thing, the engine goes completely silent and you think you've stalled or been punctured by a crab; for another, the thing that is impossible to make completely waterproof is the clutch : we had been told over and over and over again : whatever happens, *don't de-clutch*. There was the most agonising, compulsive longing in my left foot to do just that thing. In the silence (apart from the noise of the shelling from both sides) it was difficult to realise that the jeep was making any headway; but I looked back and there was quite a nice little wash behind us; soon the sea-level had gone down almost to the belt on my battle-dress and the pigeons were rather tetchily drying themselves out. When we landed on the beach (which for some ridiculous reason was called Roger) the water cascaded off the jeep as though it was a collie dog coming out from a swim, and the photographer went so far as to say, "Paris, here we come !" As I drove the jeep up the beach to the first gap I could see in the sand-dunes, we came face to face with the body of a Commando sticking out of a bank of sand and facing out to sea. He couldn't at that time of the morning have begun to stiffen; but one arm must have been held up by the angle at which he had been hurled into the dunes; it seemed to be pointing out across the Channel as though he was saying, "That's where I came from, and for bloody well what?" I know I dramatise (it is my job); but I kept thinking of the other youngster I'd caught on his knees half-way across, and hoping he wouldn't end the same way. At that moment a small formation of Messerschmits came in very low over the whole stretch of the beach and strafed the living bejesus out of us. I dived behind the still smouldering remains of someone else's jeep; this went up in flames almost as soon as I got to it and I had to move on quickly. I had yelled to the photographer to take cover, for God's sake; when I looked round gingerly he was standing bolt upright about fifty yards away, calmly taking photographs. He still looked worried, but I realised later that he just had a worried look. The last time I saw him was after he had been demobilised at Uxbridge; he looked more worried than ever.

A disadvantage of being one of the very few people wearing R.A.F. uniform, at any rate on our sector of the landing area, was that throughout D-day and indeed for the next day or two we were not officially attached to any larger unit and no-one seemed to want to know. When I say the very few people wearing R.A.F. uniform, I mean, of course, on the ground; there were any amount of us up above. We were officially called No. 1 R.A.F. Beach Squadron, and in the early days were supposed to come under 21 Army Group; but no-one on or near the beaches knew where 21 Army Group Headquarters, if it existed, was. Or really cared. On the evening of D-day I met up quite by chance with a permanently cheerful Squadron-Leader called Dobby, who had landed before me with the Commandos; his job was to make as quick a recce as possible and signal back informing the Tactical Air Force H.Q. whether there was any air-strip on which at least some light aircraft could land right away. He told me, with a merry laugh, that there wasn't. He had built a sort of dug-out in the dunes, using some Norman's blown-off door as a roof; considering everything, it was really quite comfortable, and I had my first real meal of the day in it. The Mars bars had gone earlier, and the shortbread had got soggy in landing. We had been equipped with what in the previous difference of opinion were called iron rations, plus a neat little stove gadget and matches, all waterproofed like the rest of the gear. The meal was surprisingly good; not perhaps up to the standard of the Ivy or the Savoy, but we were hungry. The worried photographer—he was a corporal —had bedded down by himself in a dip of the dunes some little distance away; inverted snobbery. The Squadron-Leader and I had told him, "Don't be ridiculous, for God's sake : come *in*," but he apparently considered it wasn't his place. During the day I had made a number of recordings, and I also recorded the Squadron-Leader's impressions of his own landing. Being interviewed by the B.B.C. for 'War Report' struck him as hilariously funny; he could hardly get through the recording for giggling. I kept going down to the beach-head and trying to persuade the Navy types to take the recordings back with them on their return trips; until a few days later when we got organised and a transmitter was set up, this was the only hope we had of getting them back. The B.B.C. had arranged a highly efficient network of collectors at all the South Coast ports who would snatch the discs (the portable recorder was an old-fashioned disc job with a battery and, if that failed, a cranking handle) and whisk them up to London. Some of the recordings made it and some didn't; one couldn't really blame the Navy for failing to put the Carter Paterson job high in their priorities. They had other things and people to deliver.

Another disadvantage of wearing the pale blue gear was that as the day progressed and one kept on flattening oneself in the sand and then getting up and dusting oneself down, the pale blue began to look more and more like field grey. We were therefore shot at regardless, not only by the enemy snipers still in the shelled or burnt-out remains of the little houses on the edge of the coast where the French had enjoyed their summer holidays, but by our own side. Sometimes I thought our own side was the more dangerous.

There was a wonderful sunset that evening. I was standing at the entrance to the dug-out during a lull in the shelling when the most almighty roar of aircraft brought everyone out of their holes. Two great waves came in from the sea; the first of glider-towing bombers, the second bringing the paratroops. The bombers released their gliders and they slipped gently down between our own positions and the first rising slopes of the ridge of hills ahead of us. The bombers swept majestically round; it seemed quite slowly as though they were lingering on purpose in the hope that the Luftwaffe or the enemy ack-ack would have a crack at them. Then, seemingly disappointed, they turned out to sea and went home for their suppers. The aircraft carrying the paratroops did exactly the same; they swept over our heads and the parachutes began to drop just at the foot of the ridge. They opened and billowed out : hundreds of them, pure white against a lovely sky. We used white parachutes for men and coloured for supplies, and it was men we were needing that night. The troops on the beaches or the sand-dunes forgot all about the shelling and the snipers; they stood on the edge of the trenches or the holes they had dug and waved and yelled themselves silly. It was the greatest hoister of morale that could have been provided and it came at exactly the right minute. I talked next morning to some German prisoners; the arrival of those two waves of aircraft seemed to have an equally great effect on them—with the morale cascading in the opposite direction. They said they had never imagined that we possessed so many aircraft and that when they saw them—the first formations some three miles inland and the tail of the armada still out on the horizon—they knew that it was hopeless. I did a slightly hysterical commentary on the arrivals; it was broadcast after the nine o'clock news on the following night, and I am told I was more or less incoherent. I'm not surprised; I think we were all incoherent at the time.

Our dug-out was, I suppose, about two hundred yards from the sea, certainly no more. When darkness fell, the dull crumps of the armoured battle that was going on a mile or two further inland between ourselves and the German 21st Panzer Division (which had arrived smartly on the scene) seemed to be getting steadily louder and nearer. It is a very nasty noise indeed. On the B.B.C. midnight news it was announced that everything had gone according to plan and that Allied forces had taken possession of our first main objective, the city of Caen, which was well over fifty kilometres away and is the place where (apart from Broadcasting House that night) the tripe comes from. Dobby had lit his pipe and was pulling away at it with both hands round it to cover any giveaway glow; he gave another giggle and said, "It's news to me." Somewhere around three in the morning I was taken short and stealthily crept out of the dug-out to relieve myself. Normally this is a function which I can carry out swiftly and with the minimum of fuss; on this occasion it seemed an age before I really got into my stride. I was perhaps a quarter of the way through my stride when in the darkness a few yards ahead of me on the dunes a figure appeared and stood there motionless, facing in my direction. The snipers were still having a ball, they were pinging away from some bombed building near the sea; the tank battle seemed to be even louder and closer. I had never in my life killed so much as a rabbit; I brought out my revolver—I had managed to scrounge some correct ammunition—and I remember thinking that it was late in life to start killing and a pity that one had to start with a man, but here, I suppose, we go. I then realised just in time that the figure standing motionless in front of me was Alf, the photographer, also having a pee. The rim of the Channel was still only those few hundred yards away, and the crumps of the tank battle were definitely getting louder.

Once again, we were in; but it seemed to me only just. And there were several times that night when one wondered : for how long?

5

RELAX. THIS IS not going to be a blow-by-blow account of the entire European campaign in World War II. War bores are probably the worst kind of bores; golf bores, with any luck, can be stymied in mid-swing by around the third or fourth hole by saying, "Personally, I prefer tennis"; cruise bores can be stilled even before they have reached Las Palmas by telling them you used to go there before it was ruined by tourism. But war bores and especially bomb bores . . . ("I was walking down Shaftesbury Avenue one morning . . . it was a glorious day with not a cloud in the sky, and not a siren had sounded . . ."; who the hell wrote that?) . . . war bores, once they get under way, are the hardest to stop. I suspect it has always been so. Uriah the Hittite, I am sure, was a cracking bore about ending the siege of Rabbah; Hannibal no doubt bored the pants off his weekend house-guests by going on and on about getting those elephants over the Alps; I have an elderly relative who at the drop of a hat will re-fight Verdun without omitting one mouthful of mud; perhaps I am in danger of going the same way. The awful thing is that I enjoyed the war. If—which is unlikely—I was asked to take part in that television series 'The Best Years Of My Life', I would have to choose the war years. I am by nature a loner—I agree with whoever it was who said that the best life is a busy solitude— but it was wonderful for once to be part of a gang. But there is no need to go on about it; certainly not to the younger generation who knew nothing of the last mess-up and rightly don't want to know. There are, however, one or two strictly non-militant incidents which may be of interest. Let us skip such minor matters as the eventual capture of Caen (six weeks after the B.B.C. occupied it); the indescribable slaughter in the Falaise Gap; the morning a large formation of U.S.A.A.F. Fortresses made a slight error of judgment and dropped their entire load on the 2nd Polish Division, Hermione and my-self; and the other New Year's Day morning in Brussels when Goering—with a typical last-fling gesture—rounded up every available remaining German aircraft and caught the R.A.F. with the most monumental hangover.

In the days and weeks following D-day, the build-up of armour and supplies on our sector of the beach-head was colossal. The only thing that worried some of us was that there was not the slightest sign of an advance. I went over to 21 Army Group one morning and asked one of the Intelli-gence Officers just why. My boss "Mary" Cunningham, wanted to know, I said. ("Mary" and Montgomery did not exactly see eye to eye). "Not to worry, old man," said the In-telligence Officer. "We've got absolutely everything we need, more than we need, actually, and they're all raring to go. The only slight trouble is that the N.A.A.F.I. wagons are at the front and the tanks are at the back, and it'll take some little time to sort them all out."

Not all the ammunition and personnel that was landed in those early days remained so immobile. Early in July, on a day which had begun with a devastating Bomber Command attack on Caumont, there arrived—looking faintly green after a rather choppy crossing—the first E.N.S.A. troupe to present a straight play for the edification of the boys. The play was Frank Vosper's thriller, *Love From A Stranger*; the company was headed by Ivor Novello (just out of jail), Diana Wynyard and Margaret Rutherford. They gave their first performance on a very wobbly fit-up stage in the middle of a very large field at five o'clock in the afternoon in baking sun-shine. Canvas erections had been rigged up on either side of the stage, behind which the company changed and made up : chaps on the one side, the girls on the other. The audience consisted of some two thousand troops sprawled out on the grass at such a distance from the stage that not even the shrill shriekings of Miss Rutherford could be heard. The play has some extremely tense moments in it—why Basil Dean chose it or why Ivor agreed to play in it, I cannot imagine—and it seemed that every fly, bluebottle and midge in Normandy had got together and agreed to settle on Miss Wynyard's delectable nose in her more intense scenes. Miss Wynyard was a lovely actress, but few people can get away with a taut, hysterical bit of acting if they are continually flicking flies off the end of their nose. Worse than the flies were the aircraft. It had been a big day in the air and the effort went on until late at night. Spitfires and Thunderbolts and Lightnings and Typhoons and Mustangs dived low over the fit-up stage, came down to inspect the audience thoroughly just in case they turned out to be a concentration of enemy troops, and on two occasions some Spits did a victory roll directly overhead. The company yelled their lines at the top of their voices, even through all the more quiet and moving moments of the play, but all that was evident to the audience was distant mute mouthing. I went round back-stage after the first act to see Ivor. He was sitting on an upturned compo ration box and he greeted me with a wan smile. "I can only suppose," he said, "that all these bloody aeroplanes were sent here specially by Lilian Braithewaite."

Having survived this ordeal, Ivor and the company moved into the lovely little municipal theatre in Bayeux, where they played for a fortnight, sometimes doing the show three times a day. The play is a tough one to do even once a day; to do it at ten in the morning to an audience of men just pulled out of the front line and so worn out that it is clear when the curtain rises that at least the front eight rows are sound asleep—this is no picnic. But at the end of each performance Ivor used to step down into the orchestra pit, get at the piano, and the boys not only woke up but sang their hearts out. He used to say, "This is a song I wrote in World War I" and play 'Keep The Home Fires Burning' with everyone belting it out almost before the first bar had been played. Then one day he said, "Here's something I've just written; it's never been played before in public; let's try it out on you." And again, though they didn't know the words, the boys joined in after the first few bars. You knew that another great hit had been born. The title of the number when it was first done in that little theatre in Bayeux was 'When You Come Home Again'. Later it was changed to 'We'll Gather Lilacs'.

Long before this—on D day plus 3, in fact, Auntie B.B.C. had decided that the listeners should have some idea of the rapturous welcome being given to the Allied forces, and sent me a signal asking me to record the church bells of Normandy pealing out in joyous celebration of the liberation. This was difficult. For one thing, the Normans had given us little or no sign of welcome; they are a dour and cautious race, and quite rightly they decided to wait until it was absolutely certain that we were staying. For another thing, there were very few church steeples left intact, and the few that were still standing almost all had snipers in them. I eventually found one village where the church was more or less whole, apart from a large tear in its roof. I routed out monsieur le curé, a very clean and cadaverous gentleman who moved quickly and with a great swishing of robes; he ushered me into his study, locked the door, and I explained what I was after. If I had come one day earlier, said the curé, it would not have been possible to ring the bells; and now—malheureusement—it was only possible to ring two out of the original three. Until dusk on the previous day there had been three German snipers up in the church tower; they had given themselves up when they ran out of ammunition, and it had been found that during their stay in the tower they had broken the biggest of the three bells. Monsieur le curé pleaded with me to wait a week for the bell to be repaired; I could then record all three in their full repertoire. I said I would prefer to record the two remaining bells now; the door was unlocked and I was swished out and introduced to a very sinister individual who looked rather like Raimu. Monsieur le curé left me abruptly and vanished back into his house, locking both his garden gate and his front door after him. Raimu could not have been less enthusiastic about bell-ringing, though I gathered that this was his occupation—or one of them. Eventually, as we seemed to be getting nowhere, I brought out my revolver and said in my best colloquial Eddie Gray French, "Montez, sonnez le carillon, and toute bloody suite." He montez'd and sonnez'd very grudgingly indeed. I was sorely tempted to say in my commentary that the bells clanging out in joyful celebration of that village's liberation were only doing so because the bell-ringer had been ordered at gun-point to get up them stairs and perform. I have a strong suspicion that the German snipers were still up in the tower; if they were, I hope the ringing in their ears lasted a long time.

When, remarkably quickly, things became organised and the Tactical Air Force was able to move itself lock, stock and, where possible, a barrel or two across to Normandy, one of the joys was to tear around in Hermione visiting the different Wings. For the first few weeks everything was splendidly informal; the crews were under canvas and the Typhoons and Spitfires under apple trees in the orchards. After that, military police stopped you at the entrance and demanded to see your pass, and fussy adjutants got piqued if you didn't report first to them before talking to the pilots. But until officialdom became rife, life was free and easy and very pleasant. I remember Johnnie Johnson rushing out to me stark naked to show me a congratulatory telegram he had received from the high-ups after some successful mix-up with Messerschmits, his spaniel

Sally barking at his heel, no doubt thinking that fighter aces ought not to behave in this exhibitionist manner, at least not on the ground. My favourite port of call was 121 Wing—our leading Typhoon Wing. It was commanded by the Rhodesian Charles Green, who gave the Germans a great deal to worry about; and its well-being was cared for by a remarkable character called Tim Morice. During the Normandy activities he became a Group-Captain; the first time I saw him after his promotion he took a sidelong glance at the four narrow strips of brand new braid on his shoulders and said, "Looks like Clapham Junction, doesn't it?" One afternoon in July I went up to Camilly, where 121 Wing was stationed, to scrounge a cup of tea or with luck something stronger. Tim popped his head out of his caravan—they had become rather grand, caravans instead of tents—and said, "Good God! ... I suppose if you know, the whole bloody press knows. We'll have *Peg's Paper* and the *Exchange and Mart* here at any moment." I had not the slightest idea of what the man was talking about. In those days Air Vice-Marshal Broadhurst flew even the shortest distances in a German cub aircraft, giving everyone except himself palpitations. The A.V.M.'s aircraft hovered over the field where 121 Wing was established; Broadhurst got out and the little plane lurched perilously to starboard as his passenger followed him. It was Churchill, beaming. He wore a short American-issue waterproof jacket and a yachting cap set at a jaunty angle. The air-crew and maintenance boys sat up from their sun-bathing on the grass and surged round him, hardly believing. He got up on some crates that were hastily rounded up, and spoke in that wonderful voice and with that wonderfully simple, economic choice of words. It was a few days after a sadly abortive attempt had been made on Hitler's life. I still have the notes of what Churchill said:

"When you think that at the beginning of the war, it took five or six weeks to get three divisions ashore, and now we have ... I mustn't tell you how many, but think in terms of millions of men. In spite of the resistance of the enemy; when you think of that, you will realise what we have achieved. There was a time when we stood alone; we had, say, two hundred field guns and perhaps fifty tanks in Britain. We stood alone until mighty Russia was attacked and defended herself with such splendid vigour; until our great friends, the United States of America, joined us in the fray and became one of the leading coalitions of nations. You have been one of the great factors which have enabled us to do the things we have done. Air power. You kept down the enemy's strength; you strangled his communications; you relieved the Navy by battering at his costal defences. There are grave signs of weakness in Germany. She is being attacked from the east and the west—and from the top. They are shooting each other in Germany today ... I'm afraid I can't help that, but they are. Danger takes a toll of many lives. But it is a righteous cause for which we are fighting. This war may go on for a long time—pray God that it goes on for a short time—but it will be talked about and read about as long as men have the intelligence to speak or read."

When Churchill finished and stepped down somewhat unsteadily from the crates, Tim took a pace forward, saluted and said just one sentence. It was all that needed to be said. "Sir: may I assure you of the loyalty of every man on this airfield, and may I thank you for your words in 1940 which have made it possible for us to be here to listen to your words in 1944." I had a lump in my throat. Naturally, I hadn't brought my recording gear with me; maybe that was the reason for the lump. I don't really think so. The P.M. then adjourned to Tim's caravan for what was loosely described as tea.

I missed, alas, being occupied with the battle of the Scheldt, the liberation of Paris; but I liberated Brussels all right. Hermione was the first jeep into the Place Bruckère; we had flowers thrown at us, were more or less hi-jacked off the jeep, thrust into the nearest café, and out came the champagne. By this time I had fallen heir to a driver, another splendid Cockney character called Harry Gosling: Gossers. He literally saved my life on at least two occasions. Some years ago I was doing an 'Any Questions?' programme in Islington Town Hall when a note was given to me saying that someone called Gossers was in the audience and was there any chance of seeing me. The team on that occasion was, if I remember, Isobel Barnet, a woolly Conservative M.P., Marghanita Laski (odd, isn't it, it's always Marghanita Laski) and Bernard Levin, whom I had never met and was ready to dislike intensely: he had written some highly libellous things about me. Michael Bowen, the 'Any Questions?' producer, said, "You'll like him; he'll turn up late, of course, looking like a modest, well-mannered little Jewish boy who's been scrubbed behind the ears by his mother and told 'now, *behave* yourself'." I said, "You're joking." Mr. Levin, when he did turn up—extremely late—fitted the description perfectly. He was scrubbed, modest, and well-mannered; he even listened politely to some rather pointless stories I told during the dinner before the programme. I was quite angry. I got the note about Gossers only about ten minutes before the programme started; I abandoned Lady Barnet, Mr. Levin and the others, and had to be forcibly got up on the platform just in time for Fredde Grisewood to repeat the first question. We had a lengthy session in the local after the programme, but when we first met I said, "*Gossers*: you've put on weight," and he said, "What about you, guv'nor," and then added, "what about the jeep the night the pair of us liberated Brussels?" It was good to know that he, too, hadn't forgotten.

The Bruxellois and Bruxelloise who tugged us off the jeep in the Place Bruckère and swept us to the nearest café were a charming couple, obviously rich, and the owners of a superb maisonette on the Rue de la Régence. I, as a brave *aviateur* and all that jazz, was invited to dinner at their home that night. Gossers had other plans, and looked very shagged out the following morning. We were all a little starry-eyed to find the shop-windows lit and filled with exquisite model gowns or very rich and expensive chocolates; and the meal, after several weeks of compo rations and the inevitable sausages half-heated on their little cooker, was quite something. There were seven courses and before, between and after each we drank toasts to the Royal Air Force, the United States Army Air Force, Mr. Churchill, General Eisenhower, and me. Halfway through the meal I was taken short and repaired to the powder-room. I cannot think why, but for some reason I opened the doors of a large cupboard in the loo. On one of the many coat-hangers in the cupboard was a German officer's field-grey trench coat and his helmet. I didn't quite know what to do; we had advanced on Brussels at such speed that obviously there were still quite a number of the opposition around. And it did seem from a first glance at the city that the German occupation had not been, let us say, as arduous as elsewhere. I decided simply to go back and finish dinner; there had been talk of a bombe surprise to follow the caneton à l'orange. Two courses and eight toasts later a vehicle was heard revving up and tearing off at top speed and a couple of shots rang out from the courtyard below where I had parked Hermione. My hostess said, "Tonight everyone is crazy," and we went on eating and drinking. A few more toasts later, I was again taken short and once more repaired to the powder-room. And again, for some reason, opened the cupboard doors and looked inside. The field-grey trench coat and the helmet had gone. So, when I tottered down to the courtyard at around two in the morning, had Hermione. It took quite a lot of explaining away.

The night the Germans surrendered was without doubt the most dangerous night of all. We were by then camped in a pleasant little town in Germany called Suchteln, where we did absolutely nothing except play skittles in the alley along-side the local beer-keller; but we had Canadians alongside us and when the news came through on the radio, the Canadians got very drunk indeed, decided there was no further need for ammunition, and let it all off in our direction. Their sur-plus bullets pinged between the guy-ropes of our tents and one shattered the electric-light bulb which Gossers had fitted up in my own establishment. He was an even better scrounger than Mike; by V-E Day I had in my tent electric light, a bureau, rather a good Persian rug, and an Alsatian.

After the end of the war in Europe—Miss Gingold and company were still packing them in at the Ambassadors—there was, so far as I was concerned, genuine drama. I was sent back to London on embarkation leave, kitted out with tropical gear by Messrs. Gieves, and told that I was being posted to the Far East. This was not at all to my liking. It was clear that the whole sorry business would be over fairly swiftly, but once you get posted to the Far East it takes a long time for the machinery to go into reverse and get you back home and out. Two days before I was due to fly out, a Wing-Commander something-or-other rang me from Air Ministry (I was back in the flat in Grape Street) and said they were thinking of putting on an R.A.F. Pageant in the Albert Hall and my name had been suggested as—I quote his exact words —"A suitable wallah who might knock off the script, if that's what you call the damn thing." "A *pageant*?" I said. "I wouldn't know how to start. Anyway, I'm being posted to the Far East in forty-eight hours." "Well," said the Wing-co, "I think that might be arranged." "Oh," I said. "A *pageant*? But that is something absolutely up my street. I've written God knows how many pageants. When do we start?"

This was the luckiest break I had in the whole war. Ralph

Reader—a genius at mass-production—directed the show; fifteen hundred R.A.F. personnel of both sexes found themselves posted without explanation to a derelict airfield outside London and were drilled by Reader in an enormous hanger in the way he drills his Gang Shows; within a day or two they were behaving like Tiller Girls and had to be restrained from over-acting. I rang up Violet Loraine in Northumberland—she was by then the Honourable Mrs. Edward Joicey and a retired stately-home country lady—and said, "What about coming down and singing 'Let the Great Big World Keep Turning'—and, if you get an encore, 'If You Were the Only Boy in the World'?" Mrs. Joicey said, "What d'you mean : *if* I get an encore?" and when I brought up the question of fee or expenses, added, "Just a bottle of Scotch in my dressing-room, dear. I'll be there."

The show was a riot; that thing was dropped on Hiroshima; the need for useless R.A.F. ground personnel in the Far East faded; and after what seemed an interminable wait, I was kitted out at Uxbridge in the regulation civvy outfit of sports jacket, grey flannels, shirt, collar and tie, and choice of either a cloth cap or a trilby—in my case 6¾, and I take 7⅜ —all packed up by an obliging corporal in a large cardboard box. I caught the tube from Uxbridge and shot back to the flat in Grape Street; Jimmy Agate had died and the nights without the performance in the lift seemed strangely quiet. But, for a very welcome change, we were out.

Because, I suppose, of the success of the *Sweet and Low* revues, I was signed up on a five-year contract for London Films by Alexander Korda. The money was, to me, astronomical. I started at £5,000; there was a mutual break in the contract after two years; if we agreed to carry on, the cash went up to £15,000. There was only one snag; I never put pen to paper. On the day my contract started, I arrived on the dot of nine a.m. at the house at the end of Piccadilly which had formerly been the home of Royalty and which Korda had taken over, keen, raring to go, and with my pencil sharpened. Nothing happened. Nothing happened for several months. I used to sit gloomily in the vast circular foyer, hoping to see Alex and tell him just a few of the fabulous ideas I had for film subjects. Sitting opposite me each day, with both of us reading old copies of the *Sketch* or the *Illustrated London News*, was Sabu, the Elephant Boy. He, too, was under contract to Korda; he, too, just wanted to have a word with him. He was getting on a bit, but I think he would have been quite ready to get up on a howdah again. After about nine months of this—being, I must admit, paid handsomely and meticulously at the end of each month—I said to Korda's general manager, Bill O'Bryen, that I was so exhausted that I needed a holiday. I had no sooner reached Cannes when a telegram arrived saying, "Imperative you return immediately stop Important assignment in Hollywood stop Regards stop Alex." I drove from Cannes to Calais overnight, stopping only to fill up with petrol, and arrived breathless and filthy the next morning in the foyer of 119, Piccadilly. Sabu was still there, reading the *Tatler*. Korda turned up about three hours later and said, "My dear Alan, you look tired: why don't you go down to the south of France?" He had completely forgotten that he had sent the telegram.

After about another nine months of this, we seemed at last to be getting down to business. Korda had bought the rights of a rather bad Italian film which had a good basic idea, in order to destroy the film and use the idea. He wanted me to write the script, Carol Reed to direct, and Ingrid Bergman and Cary Grant to star. It seemed, apart from myself, not a bad set-up. He sent Carol and myself across to Hollywood to talk the whole thing over with Cary. We stopped for a day or two in New York en route; I was staying at the St. Regis and Carol was being, I thought, a little reticent about where he was dossing down; he had just given me a phone number. On our second night in New York I came back from seeing a show at the Winter Garden in the before-mentioned state of euphoria, having seen for the first time in my life a lady called Carol Channing, who had slayed me. I switched on the radio in my room and Walter Winchell said that Carol Reed, well-known British film director and hus-band of British actress Diana Wynyard, was in New York right now and was having it off with Penelope Dudley Ward. I was outraged; I rang Carol's number several times and when at last he answered I said, in my best Scottish Presby-terian fashion, "Walter Winchell has been saying the most scandalous things about you and Penelope: you must sue." He said, "I can't sue; it's true."

I left the pair of them in New York, flew to Hollywood and arrived at Cary Grant's home in Beverley Hills before he got back from his day's work at the studios. Cary was between one of his many muddled marriages; his manservant greeted me, showed me to my room, and offered me a drink. I said I would wait for Mr. Grant. I had known him before; his real name is Archie Leitch; he comes from Bristol and is just about the nicest guy around. Once, when he was in London, I took him to a musical at the Coliseum, I think it was *Annie, Get Your Gun*. He has what the Scots call a scunner of pub-licity; the seats were booked in my name and we sneaked in just as the house lights were dimming. But somehow the news got around; just before the interval a highly excited usherette sidled up to us and said would we have drinks with Mr. Emile Littler in his private sanctum. Mr. Littler was, as always, charming; he asked Cary if he had ever performed at the Coliseum. Cary said, "Oh, yes." "Really?" said Mr. Littler. "What was the name of the show?" "It wasn't a show," said Cary. "It was a variety bill. I was a stilt-walker." He was, too. As a matter of fact, his rise to fame began not far from my home town in Northumberland. He was a chorus boy and understudying the juvenile lead in a terrible tour of

No, No, Nanette in, of all places, the Grand Theatre, Byker.
The juvenile lead was more or less permanently sloshed and
after young Mr. Leitch had played for him for several weeks
he had the temerity—like myself way back in the family
business—to ask for a rise. In fact, I think the figures were
roughly the same; he was getting three pounds a week, and
he asked for £3 10s. 0d. He was sacked on the spot, worked
his passage across to the States, was spotted by a talent-spotter,
and that was that.

When he got back from the studios that first night in Hollywood, his manservant was waiting for him at the front door
of the house with what I thought was a tomato juice at the
ready. Cary said, "Haven't you had a drink, what d'you feel
like?" and I said, "I'll have the same as you." I put it down
in one, as Cary had done; it was the first time I had ever drunk
a Bloody Mary. Mr. Grant's Bloody Maries are lethal.

When I recovered, Cary said, "Tell me all about it; what's
the story line?" It was to have been his first film in England;
he was genuinely excited. As I unveiled the plot of the pro-
posed epic, it seemed to me that he became less worked up
about the whole venture. I did my best, but it struck me that
I was losing my audience; it was like a bad matinée in Hull.
Eventually I said, "Is anything the matter?" "Yes," said
Cary. "This is the film I am making right now, here in Hollywood." Korda had omitted to check up on this possibility.

Carol Reed joined us and we stayed on for six weeks at
London Films' expense, doing nothing at all except loll
beside the pool at the Bel Air Hotel or go to riotous parties at
George Cukor's or highly respectable ones at Rosalind Russell's. Evelyn Waugh used to patronise the edge of the pool,
never to go in it; he was dressed completely in black and even
wore gloves. He was collecting material for that brilliant book
The Loved Ones, and obviously felt he ought to look the part.
They were amusing and, to me, exciting days; but the
thought of going back to that foyer in 119, Piccadilly and

finding poor little Sabu still there, getting steadily older and no doubt by now reading the telephone directory, depressed me. I asked my agent to get me out of my contract; a little tear welled up in the corner of an eye as he worked out what ten per cent of a possible £15,000 was, but he gallantly did as he was asked. We were out again and free; and very worried indeed about how to pay tax on the past two years' earnings.

Reeling back from the reception given to *Jonathan*, I thought it wise to revert to revue or, at any rate, to steer clear of the Bible except on Sundays. I wrote a show called *A La Carte*; it opened at the Savoy in June, 1948, starring Hermione Baddeley, Henry Kendall, Walter Crisham and a young French chanteur called, of all things, Marcel le Bon, who had the odd habit of lifting one leg midway through a number, like a poodle at a lamp-post. He was known to the rest of us as Fifi le Mauvais. We had title trouble about the show; in the small hours of the morning, lying in bed in the Grape Street flat, I was inspired. I wrote down the perfect title on a pad at my bedside table; when I woke in the morning it still seemed perfect. I rang Firth Shepherd, who was putting on the revue, and told him that our troubles were over. "Don't tell me over the phone," he said. "Come down to the Savoy, I'll get the press representative." When I arrived at Firth's office, both he and the press representative— and one or two others concerned with the show—were waiting, agog. "Well?" said Mr. Shepherd. "What's it to be called?" "*Butter No Parsnips*," I said. There was a longer pause than Macready ever held. "I beg your pardon?" said Mr. Shepherd. "Er—*Butter No Parsnips*," I repeated, by now beginning to lose faith. "You know: soft words butter no parsnips; the words in the show aren't soft—they're hard . . . er, *Butter No Parsnips*." The show was called *A La Carte*. I still think it was rather a good title. There was a revue some years later called *Share My Lettuce*; if you can get away with *Share My Lettuce* I fail to see what is wrong with *Butter No Parsnips*.

A La Carte included perhaps the most potentially dangerous sketch of all time; a send-up of Restoration comedy as performed from the original manuscript where all the s's look like f's. Miss Baddeley made the very most of it; she revelled in lines like "come fit on the fofa and feduce me" and had a ball with the final stanza :

Fo ends our flight and flender faga; and, thank God,

Fo alfo ends my hufband's foul fufpicions : filly fod

She had to be forcibly restrained from interpolating into the sketch the well-known musical setting of Shakespeare's poem beginning, "Where the bee sucks, there suck I."

In casting *A La Carte* I fought like a demon to get Firth to engage a youngster whom I had seen many times when I was working with the B.B.C. in Scotland. He was in a show called the *Gaiety Whirl* in Ayr; he was billed simply as Sonny and was an adjunct to a rather angry close-harmony twin-sister act. The very first time I saw him I knew the kid had talent. I persuaded Firth to give him an audition; he came down to London on a Sunday between his weekly change of programme up in Ayr; he got the job. When we were out on tour he was called up to do his national service; he never made Town. I am happy to say that he has done so on a number of occasions since. He is another nice guy; his name is Dickie Henderson.

During the prior-to-London tour of *A La Carte* we played the Theatre Royal in what is now my home town, Brighton. I watched the show on the Monday night from the back of the dress-circle; it is always satisfactory for an author to be told that there isn't a seat in the house and the management is afraid he'll have to stand. I hadn't seen the show for two or three weeks, and something had happened to it. At the end of almost every sketch or number, most of the company—led, it seemed to me, by Miss Baddeley and Mr. Kendall—manoeuvred themselves with a rather crab-like motion over to the O.P. corner and always exited on that side of the stage. On investigating the matter it turned out that there was a bar immediately opposite the O.P. exit called the Single Gulp which in those days was unwisely kept open throughout the performance. I am not for a moment suggesting that either Miss Baddeley or Mr. Kendall drank to excess; certainly never to a degree that affected their performances. Mr. Kendall enjoyed his gin; after his cremation we all ran down the hill in Golders Green to the nearest pub, ordered doubles all round, and said, "This is the way Harry would have liked it." I am convinced there is a fortune to be made in owning the nearest pub to a cemetery or a crematorium. Miss Baddeley still enjoys her brandy-boos; I like pretty well anything liquid. But in those days—the late forties—I seemed to be saddled with lushes or worse. I wrote a revue called *Sky High*; half-an-hour before the first matinée at the Phoenix Walter Crisham—who was again directing—rang me in a state of panic with the news that a member of the company had just been arrested on a somewhat unsavoury charge. He was one of those highly competent supporting players in revue who appear in different disguises in practically every sketch or number. We had had no time to rehearse the understudies, having been concerned (as one always is in revue) with running order trouble; I was the only person who knew, or thought I knew, my own words. I went on, realising very early in the afternoon that none of the young man's clothes fitted me and that I had saddled him with eighteen very quick changes for eighteen not very good parts. Some years later, the director of a terrible flop of mine at the Winter Garden called *Top Secret* did more or less the same thing on me. To be exact, he rang halfway through the first matinée of *that* disaster with the news that the leading lady had arrived stoned and was to be sacked immediately after the show. I couldn't, on this occasion, take over the part; the poor girl was playing the extremely lah-di-dah wife of the British Ambassador in some Latin American republic. A few years later the actress concerned accosted me in a Brighton pub. "I know," she said, reeling slightly, "I know they told you I was pissed on that Satinée maturday. I have news for you : I was dead cold sober. I spent the morning having my portrait painted by a very distinguished paintrait porter, and there he is—over there." At that moment, the gentleman at whom she was pointing fell flat on his face on the floor of the saloon bar and the man behind the bar said he thought he'd better get them a taxi.

In spite of the fate of *Jonathan* and the success of the revues, I was still resolved to get a straight play on. It is a much more rewarding business than even writing a complete revue; in revue, you are one of a team of contributors—the composer, the musical arranger, the designer, choreographer, the lot. When you write a straight play and it succeeds, you can inwardly purr and say, "This is *mine*." Also, of course, you don't have to share your royalties with a lot of other people. At the very end of that decade—in the autumn of 1949—I borrowed a cottage in Surrey from Elliott Mason and wrote a comedy called *Castle in the Air*. It was written specifically for Jack Buchanan; I used to speak each line of his part out loud after I had written it, trying to impersonate that unique voice of his, making absolutely sure that everything was dead right for Jack and Jack alone. I sent him the play and surprisingly quickly got a summons to meet him in his office above the Garrick Theatre, which in those days he owned. It was four o'clock in the afternoon; he received me sitting at his desk, eating a boiled egg and dry toast, with a pot of tea in front of him and a silver-grey trilby perched on his head at the inevitable Buchanan angle. He wore the trilby more or less always; he had a superstition about taking it off, and the stage management used to have to sneak up behind him and reverently remove it just before he made his first entrance in a show. He said, picking up the copy of the play I had sent him and wiping a little egg off it, "I like it, old boy. Damn funny. But of course it isn't me. I'll put it on, old boy, but I couldn't possibly play the part. Just isn't me. Sorry." It took us several weeks to convince him that it might just possibly be right for him. I think it was Coral Browne who finally did the trick. She said, "Don't be such a bloody fool, dear. Of course it's you. He's selfish; he's a liar; he'll do anything to get what he wants; he knows he's only to lay on the bloody charm to get it; it's *you* all right, dear." So for me *Castle in the Air* ushered in the fifties. A year or so ago I did a B.B.C. T.V. programme called 'Were Those the Days?': it was a nostalgic backward glance at television in the fifties ... Sylvia Peters, Macdonald Hobley, Jacqueline Mackenzie, Muffin the Mule, 'Animal, Vegetable, Mineral', 'What's My Line?' and so on. We were all hoping for a series out of it, but this failed to materialise. Perhaps the fifties weren't the days. But, so far as I was concerned, they were.

6

Touring in the fifties with a star like Jack Buchanan was not at all like going on tour today; not, alas, that there is much touring today. In the fifties in each major town or city there were at least two or three theatres in cut-throat competition with each other; no subsidies, no Arts Council grants. If the show at the King's was better than the one at the Royal or the one at the Hippodrome, the customers came to the King's. It was as simple as that, and a very good thing too. At the moment I know it is a highly unfashionable view to hold, but show business is at its best when it is competitive: if artists know they are going to be paid irrespective of results, either on-stage or at the box office, or if managements know their losses will be re-couped, there is a very real danger of them becoming permanent civil servants and of standards plummeting. Perhaps slowly; we are still in the comparatively early days of subsidising the Arts in this country; still in the first flush of excitement about new (and, in many cases, totally impracticable) theatres being built and large sums of money being made available to run them. I had a revival of a play of mine put on in an Arts Council sponsored and rate-payer aided provincial theatre two years ago; one page of the programme was a list of the administrative personnel. They numbered forty-two: the director of productions, assistant director of productions, assistant to the assistant director of productions, und so weiter. When the play was originally staged in London we had (apart from the resident theatre staff) a director, a stage manager, two assistant stage managers (who understudied and, if required, performed) and a wardrobe mistress. I think Miss Jennie Lee is a splendid lady, but I cannot help thinking of the future when all concerned know that their money is safe every Friday, no matter whether they have been good, mediocre, or bloody awful. You have only to see an average production at, say, the Comédie Française or the Theatre de la Monnaie in Brussels to recognise the rotting results of year after year of state assistance. Unaided competition is the thing: the survival of the fittest. In the early fifties, there was a list each week in *The Stage* of anything up to forty or fifty shows on tour in the provinces, each one trying to out-do the other in whichever town they were playing. In the copy of *The Stage* for the week in which I am writing, there are three: one is the Festival Ballet at Eastbourne, *Ten Little Niggers* is at Weston-super-Mare, the third is a play at the Rex, Wilmslow. Something, I feel, has gone wrong and it is not solely due to the box.

Mr. Buchanan toured in style. The Rolls; the chauffeur; the best hotels. He also worked in the grand manner. Halfway through rehearsals for *Castle in the Air* he suddenly announced that he was going to New York. Rehearsals had been uneasy; Jack was having trouble with his lines; he was not what is known as a quick study. We were all plunged into the depths of despair; we decided we would never see him again, certainly not in *Castle in the Air*. He left us on a Friday and turned up again for rehearsal at ten o'clock on the following Monday, on the top of his form. He even knew the first act. In the lunch break someone asked him why he had gone to New York. He said, "Didn't I tell you? I got married." Coral Browne, who was playing opposite him in the piece and was besotted about the man, pushed her plate to one side and said she couldn't think why but she had absolutely no appetite. For some reason Jack was ridiculously reluctant to bring the two ladies together; the new Mrs.

Buchanan was not allowed to come to Bournemouth, where the tour opened, and it was not until the middle of our second week—in Edinburgh—that Suzy said to me, "This is crazy. I *must* meet her." I took her to Coral's dressing-room, they both said, "well! ..." simultaneously, became the greatest of friends, and have remained so ever since.

The following story is told only to try to explain why stars are stars. There was one line in the play which should have got a laugh; Jack had failed to raise a titter on it all week in Bournemouth and it was beginning to get him down. The play was a bit of nonsense about an impoverished Scottish earl who owned a very damp castle in Aberdeenshire and was faced with the option of the stately home being requisitioned by the National Coal Board as a hostel for disgruntled miners or being bought outright for a vast sum by a rich and comely American heiress. The Coal Board representative, played by William Kendall, when making preliminary enquiries about the property, had to ask how many bedrooms the joint contained. "Forty-eight," Jack had to say. "Running water in all?" enquired the Coal Board. "In some cases," Mr. B. had to reply, "only down the walls." It is not a brilliant *bon mot*, but it *should* have got a snigger, even in Bournemouth. On the Monday afternoon in Edinburgh, I went to the box-office to collect some tickets for those members of my clan who had written saying they wished to support me, and were sure I could get them comps; for some reason, after paying hard cash for six stalls, I walked through the foyer to the back of the pit. The theatre was in darkness; Jack was alone on-stage under that same single cruel working light. I sneaked down into a seat around row S just as I had done on that terrifyingly wet morning at the Comedy Theatre in London, and sat there—fascinated. For an hour and a half he said that one line—"in some cases, only down the walls"—in every imaginable inflection or permutation of inflections. Sometimes firmly, sometimes throwing it away, sometimes ponging it out front, sometimes almost dismissing it. Then he placed his right shoulder square to the footlights and to where the audience would be, made a sharp downward gesture with his right arm indicating all that damp cascading down the walls of my terrible old castle, and walked briskly off-stage. He never, either that night or during the year's run of the play in London, got the end of the line out; the laugh came instantly through the picture he painted in that gesture of that dank, soggy wall. This is stardom: it almost always means hard work, and it is something that makes an author very grateful indeed when he has the great good fortune to have a star like Buchanan to put across his lines.

Miss Browne, as soon as she had read the play, hastened to Norman Hartnell and caused to be built a full-length evening gown for Act Two which even in those days cost a fortune. She was playing the impoverished Earl's even more impoverished housekeeper and according to the plot, if one may use a loose expression, had not been paid any wages for several weeks if not months. The gown had a very wide flared skirt with a large centre panel which was completely encrusted with sequins and embroidery; it was the sort of thing the Queen Mother wears superbly, but it really wasn't totally right for a financially harassed housekeeper in the Highlands. She made her entrance in it coming down the stairs (in those days we had stairs, French windows *and* plots) looking a million dollars; she was absolutely mad about it. After the Saturday night performance in Bournemouth we were all having supper and the inevitable post-mortem at Jack's table at the Branksome Towers Hotel. Jack was discussing golf with Bill Kendall; he was now having trouble, not with his lines, but with his swing. He was, of course, a master of the throw-away line; he certainly threw one away beautifully that night. He half-turned to Coral, said, "Oh, by the way, old girl, get rid of that frock" and then went on talking to

Bill about approach shots and slices. Miss Browne was red-eyed for weeks. With his usual generosity, Jack told her she could have the dress as a present; Miss Browne, still smouldering, said she never wished to see the bloody thing again in her life, and it went back to the wardrobe. Coral went off and bought a simple little black number more befitting her role; I think it only cost around a hundred and twenty guineas. Two years later, having stopped smouldering, she asked Jack if she might borrow the Hartnell number for a New Year's Eve party in London. Jack said, "Well, of course, old girl; I told you—take the damn thing." Miss Browne, ethical as ever, said no : just to borrow it for the one evening. During the party someone dropped a lighted cigarette in the middle of the centre panel; it wasn't noticed for some little time until Miss Browne started smouldering again, and it didn't improve the panel one little bit. There is obviously a destiny that shapes, not only our ends, but our centre panels. The dropper of the cigarette was Norman Hartnell.

For me, *Castle in the Air* ushered in the fifties, though actually it opened in London at the Adelphi in December, 1949. Before the curtain rose on the first performance there was a remarkable attempt by two representatives of the Coal Board to have the play banned. (The Coal Board was by no means the hero of the play.) They were told politely but firmly that once the Lord Chamberlain had given his licence to a play, no-one could stop it being performed. (I am by no means sure whether the abolition of this safeguard is a good thing.) The Press, naturally, were alerted; the alleged banning attempt was front-page news in all the morning papers and gave us thousands of pounds of free publicity. Not that we needed it; the notices were unanimous raves and the show ran for just under three hundred performances. And the Adelphi is a very big theatre for a light comedy with only five characters. I have never been absolutely sure whether the banning attempt was really the work of two very stupid and officious officials, or a crafty publicity stunt thought up by Jack.

The next great star to brighten the decade for me was Ivor Novello. I had known him for many years—even before that unglamorous first night in that field in Normandy—but I was more than a little taken aback when he said he was writing a new musical and wanted me to do the lyrics. I am not, after all, everyone's idea of a romantic lyricist and until then Ivor had almost always had the same lyricist: Christopher Hassall. The show was *Gay's the Word*; it was the end product of a promise Ivor had made many years before: one day he would write a musical for Cicely Courtneidge. I was naturally thrilled, and a little apprehensive. To begin with, I assumed that Ivor would want to write the score first and I would have to fit the words to the music; until then, in the revues, I had always craftily got the words in first and left the composer to do the fitting. Not at all, said Ivor; just let me have your lyrics and I'll see what I can do with them. This was for me an education. I fed Ivor each lyric as it came off the assembly-line (he had written a draft of the book, indicating where each number should crop up) and he wrote the score usually on Sunday mornings at *Redroofs*, his country house near Maidenhead. I have never known any composer work so quickly or get what was almost note for note the finished version of a tune the first time he played it on the piano. The only thing that held him up was the fact that he enjoyed sneezing; he used to tickle the inside of his nostrils with a toothpick or the non-operative end of a matchstick until he started to sneeze. Once he started he took a very long time to stop, during which I stood by waiting to get a lyric in edgeways. The man oozed tunes; they were packed inside him like clothes in a bulging suitcase at the end of a long holiday. He also had a very shrewd assessment of a lyric. I remember handing him the lyric of one of the numbers in *Gay's the*

Word and saying, "I'm sorry; you said you wanted a waltz here, and this could never be a waltz." He sat down at the piano, put his spectacles on the end of his nose, looked at the lyric for at the most thirty seconds and said, "It could, you know, if you cut out every third line." I was outraged: cutting out every third line of my deathless prose, indeed. I then put *my* specs on the end of *my* nose, peered over his shoulder, and realised that the operation made the whole affair very much neater and better.

The hit number in *Gay's the Word* was a very long and wordy saga called 'Vitality' which ended the first half. It really did go on and on. When we had written it, we invited Cis Courtneidge to hear it in Ivor's flat in the Aldwych. It was early afternoon; Ivor asked Miss Courtneidge if she would like a cup of tea. "No, no," said Miss Courtneidge typically. "Let's get down to work." Ivor played the number and I, Heaven help me, sang it. It really was a pill, and a great deal more difficult than any present-day pill taken orally. It lasted at least twelve minutes and, even before hearing it, Miss Courtneidge was well aware that it was to be accompanied by a hectically strenuous dance routine with the full company. (At the final dress rehearsal, which only ended because they had to open up the theatre to let the first night audience in, one of the dancers—Denny Bettis—fainted clean away and I had to half-carry him across to the Marquis of Granby and give him a brandy.) When I finished doing my best to put the number across and sank into an armchair, sweating profusely, Miss Courtneidge said, "M'm . . . I think I *will* have a cup of tea, dear." On the first night of *Gay's the Word* at the Saville in February, 1951, something extraordinary happened. London first night audiences have at least two idiosyncrasies: they are very slow indeed in being persuaded to take their seats for the rise of the curtain, and they are remarkably swift in getting to the bars in the interval. On this occasion, when the curtain came down after 'Vitality' at the end of the first half, no-one in the theatre made a move in the direction of the bars. They just stood up and cheered and cheered and cheered. We had another smash hit on our hands; the show ran for just over five hundred performances. And the Saville, too, is a big theatre.

While *Gay's the Word* was on tour prior to London, Ivor was playing in *King's Rhapsody*. He was ill and tired and obviously in need of a holiday; we went to his house in Montego Bay, Jamaica. By "we" I mean some of his faithful entourage; in this case Phyllis Monkman, Adrienne Allen, Beatrice Lillie, Bobbie Andrews, Olive Gilbert and—a comparatively recent member—myself. We had a terrible flight over. It was New Year's Eve, 1951, but the flight was anything but festive. Shortly before landing at Nassau we ran into a really bad electric storm; the lightning caught one wing-tip of the plane and seemed to sizzle through the aircraft to the tip of the other wing. There were two nuns on board who kept crossing themselves, which—though I am sure it helped them—didn't cheer us up a great deal. Beatrice Lillie was sitting next to me; she said she thought she wouldn't say no to a large Scotch. She was just about to raise it to those meaningful lips of hers when the plane dropped a hundred feet or more and her drink described—as in the case of that platter of mince mentioned earlier—a parabola and landed more or less intact in my crutch. Miss Lillie, outwardly unperturbed, said, "I think I'll have another large Scotch, dear."

Montego Bay was a joy. In those days there was only one hotel on that fabulous beach called Doctor's Cove; now I believe they have even dug up the cemetery to make room for more sky-scrapers. Lord Beaverbrook owned the house next to Ivor's; there was a gap in the hedge of bougainvillea which was alleged to separate the two and around six each evening —when we were all out having drinks on the patio—that fascinating little pixie would appear through the foliage, bringing something he had dug out of his deep-freeze which he thought might come in handy for our evening meal. Olive Gilbert was in charge of the domestic arrangements; there was a certain amount of Welsh ill-feeling because Beatrice Lillie used to get up at three in the morning, raid the fridge and leave the fridge door open. Miss Lillie was also given to getting up even later in the morning and walking down to the beach stark naked; on at least one occasion I had to go after her, carry her back, return her to bed, and explain that the natives might misunderstand.

The six weeks we spent in Montego Bay were, to me, wonderful; as great a thrill as Hollywood and much, much friendlier. Gladys Cooper was staying on the island; we went to Noël Coward's house a few miles down the coast, which he had built (I suspect on purpose) halfway up a perpendicular cliff, with his own lebensraum very high up and the guest house many yards below it down the cliff, so that the guests had either to climb up to drinks or dinner as though they were scaling the Matterhorn or skid down after drinks or dinner on their backsides. We dined one night in the open air at the hotel overlooking Doctor's Cove; there was a West Indian steel band playing and Irene Castle slipped off her shoes and danced barefoot on the lawn.

When we got back to England, Ivor returned to *King's Rhapsody* and *Gay's the Word* was successfully launched. I spent the first weekend in March at *Redroofs*. Even after the holiday, Ivor was obviously still ill. On the Sunday afternoon he put his feet up and the rest of us played canasta. I got a summons to go and see him in his room. I sat on the end of his bed and he told me he was coming out of *King's Rhapsody*, that he had a wonderful idea for a new musical, that I was again to write the lyrics and that the pair of us—no-one else—would go back to Montego Bay and work together on the show. He told me the title of the show and outlined the plot. I had just bought the house in which I now live in Brighton, I was moving from the Grape Street flat on the Wednesday. Ivor and I drove back to London late on the Monday afternoon; he asked me to come to his dressing-room in the Palace Theatre during the interval and talk the whole thing over. I promised I would try to, but I was in the packing-case muddle just before removal. To my regret, I never went to the theatre; I just got on stowing the bric-à-brac into tea-chests. At around two in the morning the phone rang; it was Olive Gilbert to say that Ivor had died. The strange thing—I offer no explanation for it—is that on that Sunday morning at *Redroofs* some of us had played a rather desultory game of tennis; after it, when we were all longing for a shower and a drink, Lady Juliet Duff appeared on the scene and insisted on taking a photograph of the desultory four-some just off the court. She seemed to take an interminable time fiddling away with her Brownie; we all got slightly tetchy and Ivor started muttering, "Oh, come on, dear, for God's sake: you're as slow as Wolfit." A few days after his death Juliet wrote me saying, "I know you all thought I took an age to take that photograph . . . but what worried me was that when I looked through the range-finder or what-ever it's called, there were only the three of you. Ivor wasn't there."

When the much-loved leader of a little empire dies, the grief is so great that you do and say silly things; and, in spite of your grief or maybe because of it, you laugh. I was deter-mined that when Ivor was taken away from his flat in the Aldwych, the little entourage should not be there; there was only one thing to do—get them up to Grape Street and get them sloshed. By that Tuesday night there was nothing to sit on in the flat except packing-cases and tea-chests; no carpets, no curtains, no comfort. I decided we must have flowers: bright, gay, spring flowers. I went out and bought several pounds' worth and then found that all the vases were in the tea-chests. My own removal from the flat down to Brighton was being stage-managed by Harrods; Ivor's cremation was being handled by the same admirable establishment. After the fourth or fifth round of very large gins, in that maudlin state of near-hysteria that one gets into on such occasions, Bobbie Andrews—who was Ivor's dearest friend—said, with the tears streaming down his cheeks, "Wouldn't it be awful if Harrods got them mixed up?"

The third great star I worked with in the fifties—my God, I was lucky—was Yvonne Arnaud. I wrote a play in 1952 called *Dear Charles*. To be more honest, I adapted a play which had been a big success in Paris called *Les Enfants d'Edouard* by Marc-Gilbert Sauvajon. It was a highly amoral romp and originally, like *Castle in the Air*, was set in Scotland; there were a lot of jokes about kilts and caber-tossing. It mainly concerned a lady who had three children, each by a separate father, none of whom she had got around to marrying, but one of whom—as the fledglings were growing up and wanting to get married themselves—she felt she ought to get up the aisle and at the altar. I felt this was not quite right for a Scottish ménage (after all, my relations would be coming to see the play when it was in Edinburgh) and I put the whole thing smartly back across the Channel. In those days, adultery in the theatre was perfectly all right as long as it happened on the other side of La Manche; nowadays, unless it happens in Bolton or Stoke-on-Trent, in full view of the audience and with no holds barred and no private parts concealed, it is considered old hat. There was a certain amount of disagreement about this switch of locale; it was not the only lapse in the entente cordiale between M. Sauvajon and myself. After he realised that *Dear Charles* was a hit and he was going to receive a healthy cheque each week for a couple of years or more he asked me over to Paris for the first night of his next play. It was called *Treize à Table*, and in my view was a little bastard. The whole thing was highly embarrassing; I had been brought across at the French management's expense and was lavishly entertained; after the first performance we all repaired—management, director, the star of the show, and the author—to some extremely expensive restaurant. The food was superb and the wine flowed. At around two in the morning I was asked what I thought of the play's chances in London. Going again into my Eddie Gray French, I said, "Ici à Paris, peut-être." (It ran for over a year in Paris.) "Mais à Londres," I added, making all the necessary gestures, "jamais: pas trois nuits; pas deux nuits; mais *un* nuit." I got the gender wrong; even I should have known that a night in France is female. Oddly enough, the English adaptation was done by someone else. It was presented by Emile Littler at the Duke of York's, and got the most scurrilous notices. I was walking down St. Martin's Lane the morning after it opened and a sad little man was scraping the posters off the front of the theatre. It lasted exactly une nuit. I felt somehow guilty; I hadn't meant to be so exact about its chances.

Yvonne was an enchanting and remarkable character. She was the one actress I have ever worked with who genuinely had no nerves, not even first night nerves. Many actors maintain that they don't have butterflies in their stomachs on a first night; they are either bad actors or liars. Yvonne was the exception. During the run of *Dear Charles* she would sit in her dressing-room guzzling rich, gooey gateaux (she was a secret eater) with the call-boy battering on the door and shouting, "Act One beginners, Miss Arnaud, *please*! ..." and, not yet even changed, she would say to me—daintly wiping the remnants of her last slice of gateau from the corners of her lips—"Let them wait, silly poops: they 'ave paid ... I 'ope." Her maltreatment of the English language got steadily worse, I suspect by design, the longer she stayed in this country; and her stay here began the year after I was born when she was a sort of infant prodigy pianist and to the horror of her parents went to audition for George Edwardes and landed a part in *The Quaker Girl*. Before coming to London, we toured *Dear Charles* for several months; every afternoon Yvonne, Charles Goldner, Murray Macdonald, who had directed the play (superbly), and I played canasta in Yvonne's room in her hotel. We were in Leeds one week, at the before-mentioned Grand Theatre, but doing very much better business than poor *Jonathan*. An aged floor-waiter steered in the tea-trolley as usual at four-thirty. It was the inevitable station hotel mixture; three different kinds of sandwiches, a plate of tepid little scones, even those repellant bright green iced cakes with sprigs of angelica on top. We pecked away, not really interested in the food, while we continued playing. When the floor-waiter (whom Miss Arnaud had christened Bromley-Davenport after an ancient and revered actor who was only just alive at the time) re-appeared to collect the trolley, Yvonne said, "Wrap up what we 'ave left in that serviette, mon cher; later I give it all to the gulls." Leeds is well inland; gulls are scarce. I still have the pleasureable picture of Miss Arnaud sitting up in bed after the show, stuffing herself with the left-over sandwiches, the cold scones, even those awful little green iced cakes with the angelica on top.

She lived in a village in Surrey with the unfortunate name of Effingham Common; the stage hands used it as an expletive. When anything went wrong, they said, "Oh, Effingham *Common!* . . ." and made it sound much worse than the real thing. After each night's performance, Yvonne took a train to Effingham from Waterloo. She had throat trouble (hence some, if not all, of the famous squeaks and gurgles) and one bitterly cold night in the second November of the run she got into the compartment of her train enveloped in layer after layer of woollies: cardigans, jumpers, scarves, the lot. She was completely invisible : just a vast square mass of wool. Just as the train was leaving, a young couple got into the compartment and sat down opposite her. They had been to the show and to begin with all went well, they had apparently enjoyed it. The young man then began to tell his girl friend some of the more intimate details of Miss Arnaud's private life. She had, he said, been living in sin for eighteen years with Tom Walls. (Miss Arnaud had, in fact, been happily married for considerably longer than that to a delightful pig-farmer called Hugh McLellan.) The young man, warming to his theme, missed not a detail of the way these flighty French actresses carried on off-stage, especially this one. Behind the layers of woollies Yvonne was lapping it up; then to her chagrin she realised that the train was slowing down and the couple preparing to get out. She couldn't resist it; she wove a way through all the layers of scarves and said, "Excuse me ... it's been very interesting, but I 'appen to be Yvonne Arnaud." The young man stared at her for some moments with a completely blank expression, and then turned to his companion and said, "Come on, Doris, the old cow's plastered." " 'E didn't even *recognise* me !" Yvonne squeaked when she recounted the incident next evening.

The play ran at the New Theatre for over four hundred and fifty performances, and could have run for many more had Yvonne not been ill and the public grew chary of seeing that ominous little notice pinned up at the box-office saying, "owing to the indisposition of ..." It ran for two years in Australia and New Zealand with Sophie Stewart in the lead, and for about a year in New York—under the title *The Bargain*—with Talullah Bankhead. I never saw the New York production; I am told Miss Bankhead gave the whole thing what was politely described as a new dimension. I went to her house in Connecticut one Sunday. I had been asked to come and see her about another play of mine. The first shock was that the door was opened by Zasu Pitts, who was looking

144

after Miss Bankhead—a full-time job if ever there was one. The house was filled to overflowing with very good-looking young men; Talullah said to one of them, "Dahling, let's see *Lifeboat*," and we spent the whole afternoon sitting on the floor watching the Hitchcock film she had made a few years before. When it came to any part of the film which Miss Bankhead particularly liked (always her own scenes) she said, "Run it back, dahling; let's see that bit again." I left without ever mentioning the play; Zasu showed me out and said mournfully she hoped I'd had a nice afternoon.

In a way, I am rather glad I didn't see Talullah in the part. I have seen a number of actresses playing it; all they do is remind me how incomparable Yvonne was. I saw the play once in rep somewhere on a Monday night; the leading lady skipped nine pages in the first act, cutting out all the explanation of the three fathers to their three children and rendering the rest of the play incomprehensible. There was no way of getting out of the situation; the poor soul could hardly say—when hitherto unmentioned fathers started turning up all over the place in Act Two—"Oh, by the way, I forgot to tell you . . ." I left the bewildered audience when the curtain came down on a very truncated Act One, and went and had a stiff Scotch and a poached egg. It seemed the only thing to do. *Dear Charles* to me will always mean one person only: Yvonne Arnaud. She was a warm, chuckly, very lovable woman.

To counteract any idea that the fifties, so far as I was concerned, were just a long succession of smash hits, let us gloss over—almost as quickly as they opened and closed—an alleged comedy called *Top Secret* starring Hugh Wakefield which emptied the Winter Garden, and a play called *Devil May Care* with Ian Carmichael and Moira Lister, which kept them away in droves from the Strand. There was also a musical called *Miss Marigold* which opened at the Savoy and when we were swiftly asked to leave that theatre transferred to the Saville under such conditions of secrecy that not even the box-office knew. We had a little better luck with another musical called *Bet Your Life*, which was put on by Jack Hylton at what used to be the London Hippodrome. The stars were Arthur Askey, Sally Ann Howes, and Julie Wilson. It was a moderate success, but even so the first night had its dicey moments. Julie and Sally Ann had to sing one of the hit numbers; it was a rather tricky duet in counter-melody called 'All On Account Of A Guy.' Like 'Vitality' it went on. On the first night at the Palace it stopped the show completely; I was again standing at the back of the circle and I remember thinking, "We're okay; we're home." It had been arranged that if the number got an encore it would be picked up from the start of the last chorus. To my horror, one of the girls panicked and started the whole thing all over again from the beginning. The gallery, which a few moments before had been cheering, became what is technically known as restless; you could sense the whole house thinking, "Oh, no, for God's sake, not all over *again*." The show never really recovered from that one moment on its first night. This is the terrible thing about first nights: so many people's fates and futures depend on the one thoroughly abnormal performance and reception of a show. *Nothing* about a first night is normal; neither the actors nor the audience, neither the back-stage staff nor even the programme-sellers. (The programmes are usually free on a first night; how can you expect the programme-sellers to be normal in those conditions?) The actors are tensed up; the stalls are there more to be seen than to watch and listen; the gallery is there to make itself heard, either by cheering or booing. Maybe somewhere around the middle rows of the dress-circle there is a small stratum of near-normality, but it has not a snowflake in hell's chance against the others. Perhaps the current trend of having several public previews before the actual ordeal helps; I doubt it. If only one could open a show on the third or fourth night.

In the mid-fifties, we did a revue at the Lyric, Hammersmith, called (no title trouble this time) *At the Lyric*, a second edition of which went into the West End called (I had given up suggesting things like *Butter No Parsnips*) *Going to Town*. The cast was again led by Hermione Baddeley, ably supported by Ian Carmichael and Dora Bryan. Around the same time I had also written a comedy about television, which was coming into its own and beginning to empty theatres even more efficiently than *Top Secret* or *Devil May Care*. The comedy was called *Simon and Laura*; it was put on by H. M. Tennent, Ltd. at the Strand. Its real stars were Roland Culver and again—Coral Browne; but Hugh Beaumont, quite the most astute man in theatre management I have ever worked with, suggested that the two main supporting parts should be played by Ian and Dora. Although they had both, of course, served their apprenticeship in repertory, and appeared in straight plays for the past few years, they had made their names in the West End in revue; I was naturally delighted to have such names in the show and, as it happened, it was a typically far-seeing move on Mr. Beaumont's part to engineer their transition back to what is carelessly called the legitimate theatre. Ian made a great personal success in the show; Dora not so great—but, to be fair, she had a rather nebulous wishy-washy part and was wasted in it. We opened in Manchester, where Dora is rightly worshipped; in the small hours of the morning after the first night a very drunk Manchester dramatic critic seized me by the lapels, pinned me up against one of the tobacco-stained dung-coloured walls of the lounge in the Midland Hotel (they have been painted since), and said, "You know what you've done to our Dora, don't you? *Crucified* her, that's what you've bloody well done." I must say she has resurrected expertly.

147

Simon and Laura, I suppose, stemmed from that soap-opera 'Front Line Family'; it was about a theatrical married couple on the point of divorce who found themselves trapped in a long-running T.V. series in which they had to exude sweetness and fidelity to each other. Part of the stemming may also have come from my own early experiences in television, which were disaster. I seemed always to be employed as the woffling chairman of some quite awful semi-intellectual panel game; very soon I established the reputation of being someone who, as soon as the B.B.C. launched one of these series, could get it off the air faster than anyone else. There was a thing called 'The Balloon Game'; the members of the panel (Marghanita Laski again) had to decide if, say, Rasputin, the Marquis de Sade and Anna Neagle were up in a balloon and—because of ballast trouble or a slow puncture—one of the three had to be ditched, which one would you ditch, and why. I got that one off in four weeks. There was another, equally catastrophic, called 'Who said That?', in which Marghanita was joined by people like John Betjeman and Lord David Cecil; they had to identify the authorship of quotations I read out to them, and then say whether or not they agreed with the sentiments expressed. They were usually idiotic sweeping statements like "Punctuality is the thief of time" (Oscar Wilde). It took me all of six weeks to kill that one stone dead, but I managed. On a rather higher intellectual plane, I was gainfully employed for several months as chairman of 'The Brains Trust.' This was quite an experience. The programme went out at five o'clock on Sunday afternoon, but the ritual began with lunch in a private room at Scotts at one p.m. There I met the brains: Julian Huxley, Bertrand Russell, Lady Violet Bonham Carter, Brunowski, David Cecil again, the whole cerebella. The lunch sessions were, to say the least, stimulating; if only the B.B.C. had recorded them instead of waiting until five, by which time a slight post-prandial lethargy had set in, it would

148

have been sensational. I just sat and listened; my only contribution to the conversation was to tell the waiter how I liked my steak done. In spite of the time-lag between the last brandy at Scotts and actually going on the air, 'The Brains Trust' was a very good programme; I cannot think why it couldn't be revived today. It was calm, civilised, intelligent talk, unlike the shouting matches Saint Malcolm gets involved in when discussing either the Pope or the Pill, or both, with a rabble of egged-on interrupters. Brunowski was the craftiest of the brains; he used to give me a signal indicating that he didn't wish to contribute to the discussion on a certain question. When the three other members of the panel had done their stuff, he would give me another signal indicating that he was now ready to enter the fray. And say, with his r's pronounced as w's, "Well, of course, what the question *weally* asks . . ." and pwoceed to wap the whole thing up. He was a brilliant and very likeable man; I cannot think what went wrong with that smokeless fuel he got at.

In the mid-fifties, life in Brighton was considerably brightened by the arrival, in a house just round the corner from my own, of Gilbert Harding. Gilbert was another very lovable character; behind all that brusqueness and, on many occasions, downright rudeness, he was a softie. I have known him be insufferable—many times in my house—to someone ill-equipped to answer back; invariably next morning contrition set in with a vengeance and notes of apology and large wreaths of flowers were sent to the victim of the night before. Rather like, since this seems to be developing into an exercise in name-dropping, Norah Docker. I was losing money as usual on vingt-six et carré and zero in the casino at Cannes one night when she behaved outrageously, insulting everyone from the croupiers to the Crown Prince of Thai who had dared to sit in the seat she usually sat in. Next morning, cadging drinks from her on *Shemara*, she too was writing notes of apology all round and ordering enormous armfuls of contrition carnations. Apart from sharing this particular form of hangover with Lady Docker, Gilbert was unique. He was without doubt the greatest television personality of the fifties, and though he got a great deal of enjoyment out of it (and a good deal of money) it didn't satisfy him. Hardly anything did. He called himself a telephony, and in a way—once he had become a national figure, mainly through 'What's My Line?'—he despised how easily his reputation had been achieved. He used to admit even to envying me, of all people, only because I wrote or acted or had to rehearse and learn lines, whereas he just went on the air and was himself. It took him some little time to realise that, unlike him, I *had* to prepare in advance whatever I was going to do; until I explained the whole thing to him he would come, slightly puffing, up the hill and round the corner to my house at around eleven in the morning; I would hear a stentorian bellow of "Where is that alleged star of stage, screen and radio?" and Gilbert would be all set to sit down for three or four double gins and tell me a rather amusing story about the Bishop of Winchester. After which, dear boy, he would add, I shall tell you an even more amusing story about the Dean of St. Paul's and an acolyte. (He had told me them both on many previous occasions, but he was a difficult man to stop.) Until I plucked up courage to tell him that I really had to get on with the work and would he mind postponing his popping in until early evening, I used to hide in the boot-cupboard in the hope that he would think I was out shopping.

Gilbert was an unsuccessful, unhappy convert to Catholicism. One evening in his home in Brighton he unburdened himself to me on the subject and announced that on the following Saturday morning he was to be—in his own words —"re-embraced into the arms of Rome." "Good, Gilbert," I said. "Splendid. I'm delighted. Couldn't be more pleased. High time, too." Every Saturday morning, winter and summer, weather permitting, I play tennis; the same men's doubles on the same public parks courts in Hove; in the summer we attract quite a sizable gate of the old ladies of Hove, who get there early for the seats round the courts where they can best hear my language when I miss an easy smash or, as has been known to happen, serve a double fault. On this particular Saturday the weather began by permitting and then ceased to do so; it started to pour with rain and the four of us packed it in and adjourned to the local for a lager. Gilbert was perched, rather unsteadily, I thought, on a stool at one end of the bar. I went over and asked him how things had gone. "Don't talk to me about that, dear boy," he growled. "I went into the confessional; I confessed the lot. I said I'd done this; I'd done that. I'd been too rude and inconsiderate too often to too many people; I'd sworn too much; I'd drunk to much. A voice said, 'Why?' I said, 'Mind your own bloody business, you impertinent little pip-squeak', and here I am" —knocking back perhaps his fifth double gin since confession—"*at it again*!" It must have been one of the shortest re-embracements Rome has ever known.

He was a character; we could be doing with more like him. Characters these days seem in short supply.

In 1957 and again in 1958, I was asked by B.B.C. T.V. to do a fortnightly programme called 'A to Z.' It was a very simple, obvious idea; like so many simple, obvious ideas it proved a winner. It was merely a sort of catalogue of show business personalities and the various facets of show business, arranged in alphabetical order from A, B and C (which were easy) to X, Y and Z (which were not). I was commissioned to write the linking material, appear as compère and do the interviews, and include in each programme some quite outrageous impersonation. I said I would have to think the offer over, adding in the same breath, "When do we start?" It was one of those jobs you dream about; unless the whole thing proved a monumental flop and was sunk without trace by at the latest, say, letter C, the Corporation was saddled with me for twenty-six lovely engagements; as things turned out, because we went through the alphabet twice, for fifty-two. Well, fifty-one. Early in the second series I realised that the letter Q had no very great artistic possibilities; the only really very big stars were Anthony Quayle and the Queen, neither of whom was available. I said to the B.B.C. that I really must have a fortnight off; they didn't work out until it was too late that the fortnight I had suggested was the Q fortnight. They were livid. Unable in those non-permissive days to do a forty-five minute programme entirely about queers, they did one about quizzes. It was not a great success; I came back bronzed and slightly smug for letter R (Flora Robson, Beryl Reid, Edmundo Ros, Ginger Rogers, Ethel Revnell, Ada Reeve, Lita Roza, et al.).

'A to Z' won me—and it should have been a team award shared by the director of the show, Bryan Sears, his assistant Robin Nash, and the rest of the gang—the Television Writers and Directors Guild's award for the light entertainment personality of the year. This takes the form of a sort of death mask attached to a very heavy plinth; one eye of the death mask is open and empty and the other closed; if you stick a grape in the open eye it looks very macabre indeed. It is now used as a door-stopper in the bathroom of my house in Brighton, where in winter the draughts are considerable and one needs door-stoppers. When the awards were announced and presented at one of those annual jamborees these various Guilds have at the Dorchester, Bryan Sears and I were on Capri filming Gracie Fields for, of all unlikely letters, F. We had no idea we had won it. When we got back to Victoria we were met by Bryan's secretary, a splendid character called Maggie. "This is for you, dear," she said, handing me something in a brown-paper bag. I accepted it courteously, taking it by the top of the brown-paper bag; the award went clean through the bottom of the bag and crashed on the platform. It still shows the scars, but I am very proud to have it, even as a door-stopper. It is the only thing I have ever won in my life, apart from the trip to Canada and the Sir Walter Scott prize for English Literature at Edinburgh Academy; come to think of it, I dropped that, too.

7

WHEN THE TWO-YEAR run of 'A to Z' ended, the B.B.C. gave
me a framed scroll with the names of all the artists who had
taken part in the show. It hangs in the attic room of my house
where I either write like mad or stare morosely out to sea,
thinking that I shall never again think of anything to write
about. Counting such package deals as the Alexandra Choir,
the National Youth Orchestra, the Western Theatre Ballet,
and even Rawicz and Landauer as one name only, the list
still adds up to three hundred and seventy-seven names. Once
the show clicked, pretty well everyone who was anyone in
show business clamoured to get on it, or at least was very
easily persuaded; from Eartha Kitt to Bob Hope, from Benno
Moiseiwitsch to Johnny Dankworth, from Dame Edith Evans
to Coco the Clown. So I met, apart from many old friends, a
great many stars I would probably never have worked with.
The cast list for each instalment was by no means unimpres-
sive; in letter A first time round we had Antonio, Yvonne
Arnaud, Arthur Askey, Larry Adler, Adrienne Allen and her
children (Anna and Daniel Massey), Fred Astaire, Eamonn
Andrews, and a great many more; not a bad bill. In letter B,
Hermione Baddeley, Dora Bryan, Bernard Bresslaw, Richard
Burton, Claire Bloom, the Beverley Sisters, Kenny Baker,
the Boulting Brothers and Bambi on film. You cannot really
go far wrong with a list like that. Oh, and Alicia Markova
(B for ballerina: we cheated occasionally). And on through
the Q troubles and the final anxieties of X, Y and Z (Boris

Karloff, X for X certificate; Yana and the Yugoslavian National Folk Dance Theatre; Doris Zinkeisen and Shirley Abicair—who should have been with the A's but was craftily kept waiting until Z for zither because of the shortage of big names at the nether end of the alphabet). We also very nearly had among the Z's the American comedian Zero Mostel. He was brought into my dressing-room by Eric Machwitz just before I was due to go on and start up letter T (Sophie Tucker, Terry Thomas, Mike Todd and Elizabeth Taylor, both the Tiller Girls *and* the Television Toppers, and Heaven knows who else). In each show I had a very long alliterative introduction which scared me and when Mr. Maschwitz and Mr. Mostel arrived I was muttering this in front of my dressing-room mirror, eating a hard-boiled egg and looking at myself and thinking that surely the make-up department could have done better. Eric said, "This is Zero Mostel: the very man you need for letter Z." It did occur to me to say that the gentleman's surname didn't begin with Z and if we were planning the show that way we could have had Veronica Lake in letter V or A. J. P. Taylor in either A, J or P. Before I could say anything, however, Mr. Mostel said, "I do a very funny impersonation of a coffee percolator boiling over;" and, what is more, did it there and then while I was desperately trying to remember the opening lines of my introduction. He didn't appear in the show; I cannot think why, unless it was something I said to Bryan Sears.

Bryan directed the show brilliantly, giving it style and polish, and very sensibly putting me dimly lit and, whenever possible, behind gauze. He was inclined to have tantrums, but the end product looked and sounded good, which is what matters. His floor manager through much of the two years stint was a young man called Robin Nash, later to become a very able director himself and to be responsible for many shows I have been concerned with, such as 'The Very Merry Widow' with Moira Lister and 'Before the Fringe' with just about every intimate revue star ever invented. On the day of the final rehearsals and the actual transmission the floor manager is the most important person in the studio, whatever certain artists may think. He wears headphones all the time and not least of his arduous duties is to listen to what the director is saying—or, in the case of Bryan Sears, scream-ing—into his cans, translate this into civil and tactful phrase-ology, and pass the amended version on to the cast. When Bryan got properly worked up, sparks almost seemed to be coming out of Robin's headphones; sometimes the screaming was audible in the next-door studio; and when one had heard all too clearly, "Will you, for Christ's sake, tell Alan for the four-hundredth time *not* to stand there like an under-sexed suet dumpling and *try* to remember that when he says, or rathers fluffs, the line at the foot of page 47 *he has to move to camera 4?*," Robin would come to me with a seraphic smile and say, "Bryan says it's absolutely super; he realises it's diffi-cult, but if you could *possibly* turn to camera 4 when you have your big laugh at the foot of page 47 . . ."

In each edition of 'A to Z' I did, as I say, the most out-rageous impersonations. I cannot think how I had the nerve. They were the sort of thing that Stanley Baxter does now-adays on T.V.; except that sometimes he does me. Some time ago he took me off when I was compèring 'Before the Fringe'; I didn't see his show because I was working myself, but the following morning the news-agent and the man in the post-office and the other man in the off-licence round the corner all said, "Did you see Stanley Baxter doing you last night on the telly, guv'nor? Got you off to a T, he did: every single one of your mannerisms—never missed one." Slightly irked, I folded my arms firmly in front of the man in the off-licence and said, "But I have no mannerisms." The man in the off-licence said, "Yes, he did that, too." In my own impersona-tions I did both Armand and Michaela Denis (on one occasion having afternoon tea with both Hans and Lotte Haas and trying to outdo each other about their exploring activities; it involved a great deal of trick camera work and some very awkward changes of costume and sex); Lady Violet Bonham Carter, Chan Canasta, Fyfe Robertson (rather too often for his liking : he was easy to do) the entire teams of 'What's My Line?' (earrings and all) and 'Animal, Vegetable, Mineral' (Glyn Daniel adored it, Sir Mortimer Wheeler was not amused), Peter Dimmock, Percy Thrower and goodness knows who else. The Percy Thrower send-up was filmed in my own back garden; its main theme was what to do with garden gnomes. What to do with them, in my version of Mr. Thrower's talk, was to crunch the little perishers into as small pieces as possible with a heavy spade and then bury them. I still, ten years later, find myself digging up little bits of gnomes with the same spade with which I originally crunched them. In this series of impersonations I had a number of near-misses and the occasional out-and-out disaster, but I had one real triumph. A letter came in from a fan and was forwarded to me by the B.B.C.; the lady said she had admired everything I had ever done on the telly, but my impersonation of Joan Hammond in the last 'A to Z' programme was in her opinion the best thing I had ever done. I had got her off, the lady said, absolutely perfectly; the stance, the stature, the dignity, the charm, the voice (this was mentioned last), *everything*. I was extremely flattered and wrote back to the lady in suitable terms. There was only one slight snag : it *was* Joan Hammond, not I.

I fought shy of impersonating Gilbert Harding until I did the whole 'What's My Line?' team. He was difficult to do; there was a sort of sad gentleness mixed up in that booming, bellowing voice—just as, as a person, he was a mixture of loud and soft—and it was hard to recreate. Eventually, however, I had a shot at him—*and* Isobel Barnet, Barbara Kelly, David Nixon and Eamonn Andrews; with the help of that splendid make-up department and the wardrobe, they were child's play in comparison. I was rather pleased with my Gilbert, I felt I had really got him. What cheered me even more was that when we showed the film for the first time at the final dress rehearsal the camera crew and the other technicians on the floor passed out laughing. I even got a small round of applause at the end of the film. This is rare; camera crews are not readily given to applauding, and neither would anyone who spends long hours day after day watching the same dreary people making the same dreary mistakes. In the dinner-break before the show went on the air, I had a snack in a little Italian restaurant round the corner. When I got back to the dressing-room Bryan was waiting for me, not looking his sunniest. "I'm afraid we're going to under-run by five minutes," he said. "The 'What's My Line?' item is out." "*Out?*" I said. "But it went like a bomb; didn't you hear the camera boys laughing?" "I know," said Bryan. "But we've just heard: Gilbert Harding dropped dead about an hour ago." It was not an easy show to do that night.

Three hundred and seventy-seven star names in a single series, and I suppose there is a story to be told about almost every one of them. Again relax; let us just choose a few — not all of them from 'A to Z', but all people with whom I have worked. And since we are in the 'A to Z' era, it may be neater to put the chosen few in alphabetical order, jumping not only the Q but several other letters.

A and B would have to be Arnaud and Buchanan, both of whom we have dealt with. Except that there is one other memory of Jack, many years before we worked together and became friends. Twenty-two years, in fact, before *Castle in the Air*; my mother was living in Greenock and she took me to a matinée of *That's a Good Girl* at Glasgow Alhambra; Jack and Elsie Randolph were the stars. I think the money from the sale of the house in Berwick-upon-Tweed must have come in, because we had lunch in the Central Hotel and going down the steps outside the hotel on our way to the theatre, Mr. Buchanan—wearing a silver-grey, double-breasted suit and with the inevitable trilby perched at the inevitable angle and obviously having left things rather late —revolved through the revolving doors at speed and dashed down the steps, knocking mother over. He picked her up with immense charm, said, "I really am most terribly sorry, madame," dusted her down, and tore off to the theatre. The rumour in those days was that Jack was dying of tuberculosis, that doctors were permanently standing by in the wings, and that any undue exercise would be fatal; for an advanced case of tuberculosis he certainly moved that afternoon : I should think he must have made the stage door in thirty seconds. Mother and I saw the show from the back of the upper circle (the house in Berwick had fetched very little and lunch in the Central Hotel, Glasgow, is expensive); when Elsie and Jack did 'Fancy Our Meeting' some strange sort of levitation act seemed to happen; they didn't dance, they floated—or so it seemed—an inch or so above the stage. Mother didn't notice, she just kept murmuring, "He spoke to me ... he actually *spoke* to me." She was heart-broken when the bruise disappeared.

Another B was one of the two Richards. The two Richards— they were always known as the two Richards—were a couple of young actors who were in the repertory company which H. M. Tennent, Ltd., ran for a time at the Dolphin Theatre in Brighton. They were both taken up in a big way by Emlyn Williams and his wife; I was, too, for a time. We used to spend weekends at Emlyn's house near Didcot, and play tennis more or less non-stop all Sunday. Emlyn was the most infuriating tennis player to play against; he got everything back very high and very slowly and was perfectly willing to wait until his opponent lost his temper and slammed the ball miles out of court. I had a couple of great-aunts, Mrs. Heriot and Mrs. Huddleston, who adopted the same technique. They were Scottish women's doubles champions for so many years running that the engravers printed the ditto sign on the cup even before the championships started; they once, playing against each other in the final of the ladies' singles, maintained a single rally while the chaps on the adjacent court played a whole set; and they had the further demoralising effect on their opponents by asking, when their perspiring adversaries were screaming for iced orange juice, for a nice pot of tea.

Off-court at Didcot, when the two Richards were out of earshot, it was unanimously agreed that one of the two—Richard Leech—would go places. I am glad to say that he now seems to be in very regular employment, recently mainly acting the part of a doctor on T.V.; but there was a time when things were so bad for him that he had to go back to being a real doctor in Ireland. The other Richard, we decided, just hadn't got what it takes to be a success. The reason he is mentioned in connection with the second letter of the alphabet is that he was, and is, Richard Burton.

C could be Cochran or Charlot, Courtneidge or Coward. Except that I never met the first two, and have already mentioned the last two. So it would have to be Chevalier. In the early fifties I wrote a series of profiles—under the title of 'Melvillainy'—for the *Sketch*, the old glossy one, not the daily. Maurice was one of the victims. He was doing his one-man show at the London Hippodrome and after the show when I steered him through the autograph-seekers at the stage door to take him to supper, he pointed up to an extremely grimy third-floor window on the corner of Lisle Street and Wardour Street. "You see that window up there?" he said, both to me and the hunters. "The first time I came to London, as a very young man, I stayed in that room. It was—how do you say it?—my deegs. I paid seventeen shillings and sixpence a week, in those days, for me, a lot of money. And I saw the show 'ere at the London 'Ippodrome—

it was George Robey—from the gallery (already, although I was so young, I was singing in the little music-halls in Paris) and I say to myself 'One day I will come back and appear at the London 'Ippodrome.' And to come back and be on that stage in there all alone is *won*derful!" "*Won*derful!" was said with the accent well and truly stressed on the first syllable, the arms outstretched, the grin, and the lower lip sticking out; if he had had his straw hat I feel sure he would have burst into 'Louise' there and then on the pavement in Lisle Street. He chose the most unnervingly expensive dishes on the menu and said I was not to worry about ordering a bottle of wine; as a good Frenchman he would stick to double Scotches. The *Sketch* was paying me twenty guineas a profile; the bill, if I remember, came to around fifteen pounds, plus tips. It was worth it.

D and E could be that great and gorgeous actress, Dame Edith Evans. I also did a profile of her; she came to dinner in the flat in Grape Street and I was very nervous; I had not a very good cook-housekeeper and it was saddle of lamb and I was afraid she would serve it up with either tartare sauce or gentleman's relish. I asked Dame Edith all the usual asinine questions; she suddenly said in that glorious escalating voice, "You know what I am proudest of? Being a seamstress. I began life as a seamstress; I learned my job as a seamstress; I think I am still a very good seamstress." Someone should write a part for her including the word "seamstress" towards the end of Act Two. She would make even more of it than she did with Wilde's handbag.

F: Fenella Fielding. I once, in a T.V. play by Marty Feldman and Barry Took, played the part of a chaise-longue on which Miss Fielding got up to a great deal. It is the only time I have ever played a chaise-longue; I was sore for weeks. G, apart from Gingold (if you can get apart from Gingold) would have to be Gielgud. This superb actor is a man dedicated to the theatre; he has little interest in anything else.

There is a story, no doubt apocryphal, that when some time ago Sir John came back from Vietnam and was asked what the situation was in Saigon, he said, "I've no idea, the theatre was closed." H : Bob Hope. When he appeared in what was supposed to be a pre-filmed interview with me on 'A to Z', I was held up doing re-takes on some other filming job at Ealing. I arrived breathless at the Maida Vale studios just as Bob and his entourage were leaving. He said, "Not to worry, kid; I've filmed all the answers. Just you fit in the questions." I did this live with Bob replying on film; no-one noticed.

Jump to K : Korda again. I once watched fascinated as he came down the steps leading to the sea at Eden Roc on Cap d'Antibes, arm-in-arm with Orson Welles. They were both corpulent, both smoking outsize cigars, and both deep in earnest conversation. I was lying on the raft about a hundred yards out; as their two pot-bellies became gradually sub-merged as they went slowly down the steps, I wondered what they would do with their cigars. At the last possible moment, they both threw them nonchalantly into the Mediterranean and set out for the raft in a sploshing breast-stroke. Simul-taneously a thick scum of brown nastiness spread from the rocks below the Hotel du Cap and advanced slowly towards the raft. I am sure it must have all been sorted out by now, but in those days things could go wrong with the plumbing down there; nothing, of course, to do with the Hotel du Cap, perish the thought, but if someone pulled a plug in Eze, everyone's excreta from Beaulieu to Ste. Maxime came out elsewhere. Alex and Orson did their breast-stroke back through the slime; I was marooned on the raft until the excreta passed it and was last seen heading for Algeria. I have seen Korda wearing even less than on that occasion. When I was under contract to him he was staying in the Dorchester (the Oliver Messel suite, naturally); Carol Reed and I, who were both feeling frustrated at not being allowed to get down to work, used to walk round the block before seeing him;

rehearsing what we were going to say to spur him into action. One night just as we arrived, very worked up indeed, his doctor was shown out as we were ushered in. Alex greeted us completely naked. "My dear Alan," he said, "you will have a gin and tonic. My dear Carol, you will have a Scotch. I have just had a shot up the arse." Instead of saying, as we had planned, "Now see here, Alex," the three of us sat down and had a very pleasant session, with Korda still in the currently fashionable state of nudity.

M: Mario. Mario was the genius who presided over the Ivy Restaurant; he was one of the greatest and certainly the kindest restaurateur in the world. When Noël Coward was just beginning to make a name for himself, it was Mario who saw how big the name was going to be; it was Mario, if the young man was a little short of cash, who didn't bother over-much about the bills. He was equally good to me. He and his vast, cuddly wife lived in a house in Highgate; you would have thought that having worked long hours all week making people sublimely happy with superb food and drink, the last thing Mario would have wanted on his Sunday off was to entertain, let alone get over the hot stove. But no, Sunday was his gala day; we were invited to the house, Mario cooked the meal himself; all the most expensive delicacies that had been off the menu at the Ivy on Saturday night were on the menu chez Mario on Sunday. After lunch, sometimes as early as five p.m., we went unsteadily out to the back garden and played bowls. There was an unfortunately placed little stream at the foot of the garden; most of the bowls ended up in it and were left there. We then returned to the house for drinks; Mario brought out his guitar and Madame, after an agreed period of persuasion, coy refusal, and eventual reluctant consent, sang Neapolitan folk songs in a gorgeous contralto voice deep enough to make Olive Gilbert sound like Minnie Mouse. One Sunday Mario steered me to the station to catch the last tube; in the course of the day the station had unaccountably moved. In the morning it had been definitely there, only a few hundred yards from Mario's house, but neither of us could find it at all. The only sensible thing to do was to go back to the house and bring out the guitar and the Courvoisier again. I stayed until the Tuesday; it was a really excellent lunch. Mario has now retired and he and Madame live on Lake Garda; if they are having one-tenth of the happiness there that they brought to their many friends in their home over here, they must be very happy indeed. I certainly hope they are.

Q; oh, hell. Except that I was once nudged by the Queen Mother. Stand by for the real name-dropping; what has been dropped up to now is as immaterial as an aspirate. I was invited to an informal little dinner party at Oliver Messel's; it is the sort of thing that happens to me, perhaps as often as once in a lifetime. The guests were the Queen Mother, Princess Margaret, Viscount Snowdon, Mrs. Emlyn Williams, Terence Rattigan and myself. After dinner Oliver took the Queen Mum and myself up to be shown round his studio. This was a clutter; Mr. Messel is not one to throw things away in a hurry. Among the conglomeration of sets designed ten years before for Covent Garden or sketches for some Cochran revue of an even earlier decade, we were shown the model of his latest assignment. This was a reconstruction job on some stately home in the Midlands; it included an orangery and the Queen Mother said that was what she'd always wanted: an orangery. She then asked who the reconstruction work was for. "They're very rich industrialists in the Midlands, ma'am," said Oliver. "The Watkins." "Really?" said that splendid and enchanting lady, and then turned to me and gave me the nudge. "We must get in touch with the Watkins," she said.

R: Beryl Reid. I have had the good fortune to work with almost all the great revue comediennes of the past quarter of a century: Gingold, Baddeley, Binnie Hale, Bea Lillie,

Florence Desmond, Dora Bryan and many more. I hope it will not cause the other ladies to order the large-size tin of Umbrage; Beryl, in my view, is the much under-estimated greatest of them all. To be a star in revue you have got to be much more than just a good actor; often in a three- or four-minute sketch, you have to establish and put across a definite character, with all that character's foibles and peculiarities, the building up of which in a straight play might take a whole act. Beryl, of course, as was proved in *The Killing of Sister George* (the play, not the film), is very much more than just a good actress. As far as London was concerned, she had for a long time an unhappy career; she was a well-known and highly successful artist in the big provincial summer shows and pantomimes, her Marleen and Monica were national figures; but she kept trying to be accepted as something more than this in the West End and her first three or four shots were botch ones. Each time she said, in her Birmingham accent, (she is actually Scottish) "Oh, well, that's loife, dear" and went back to earning far more in Coventry or Liverpool than she would ever earn on Shaftesbury Avenue. I don't think I helped, except perhaps indirectly, by writing a revue for her called *All Square*. It ran, or tottered, at the Vaude-ville for a few months in 1963. The timing was premature and it was largely my fault; I thought the pendulum was swing-ing away from the Fringe-type sort of intimate revue with four clever young men in polo-necked sweaters and no scenery; I thought the time was ripe for a return to an intim-ate revue with chic clothes and attractive scenery and a bit of glamour. The show, and particularly Beryl, got a rave press; but the pendulum clearly hadn't swung far enough and the clientèle stayed resolutely away. Beryl again went sadly back to the provinces. The one consolation I got out of it was that I think the show helped at last to convince a lot of people that she really was a West End star and that if she ever wanted to she could forget Marleen and Monica. She was superb; every part she played was a real person, not a caricature or a grotesque. There is a strange sort of recipe in devising intimate revue; one of the inexplicable ingredients in the dish is that the leading comedienne, having had them rolling in the aisles all evening, should suddenly still the congregation by doing a serious number or sketch about three or four items from the end of the show. It is a very difficult thing to do, especially in the case of *All Square*, where Miss Reid had to appear in a W.R.E.N. officer's uniform and the audience sat back ready for another belly-laugh. She stilled them in a matter of seconds and all through the item—it was a sad little monologue about a woman whose life had gone very agley—there was not a sound in the house until the applause cracked out after the long silence she held at the end of it. She is another perfectionist; she worked and worked on that monologue; the first time I knew she had got it absolutely right (and knew by her face that she knew) I dashed backstage, kissed her, and told her so. She said to Charles Hickman, who had directed the revue, "Alan came charging through the pass-door the minute it was over, and you should have seen his little face." For the rest of the regrettably short run of the revue I was known as Little Face. It is not, as may have been noticed by some viewers, all that little. In fact, it only just manages to fit a twenty-one inch screen.

S : Sargent. He, too, was in 'A to Z'. I met him to discuss the preliminaries in his flat behind the Albert Hall, with his budgerigar sitting on his head and one of his secretaries arranging a fresh carnation in his buttonhole. We filmed the interview with him in front of the Albert Memorial; there is a frieze of famous composers round the base of that odd erection and he was very particular indeed about which composer should share the camera with him, even in the background. To his musical genius, Sargent added a great sense of theatre; during the war when, to his credit, Jack Hylton put on a series of symphony concerts at the London Coliseum,

Leslie Banks was cajoled into taking on the spoken part in one of those works with narrator and orchestra, no doubt it was *Peter and the Wolf*—it usually is. It is a terrifying experience; having done it, I know. I once was the narrator in a lesser work called *Tubby the Tuba*; I didn't sleep for nights before the performance or, if I did, I had nightmares about cueing in the wood-winds instead of the cellos on the twenty-ninth bar after letter B on page 18. The ordeal was in no way lessened by the fact that we rehearsed in the Guildhall, where the orchestra had given a lunch-time concert, with both Gog and Magog looking down at me disapprovingly. After his rehearsal on the London Coliseum occasion, Mr. Banks asked Sargent what he should wear and what make-up. "Make-up?" said Sir Malcolm. "My dear fellow, this is a concert, not a theatrical performance." When the time came for the off, the wretched narrator—now shaking and looking much more pale and wan than he usually did—was standing in the wings and was joined by Sir Malcolm, wearing the lot. "I thought you said no make-up," said Mr. Banks. "It's different for me," Sir Malcolm explained. "The lights are on me."

T. There were three train journeys which also conveniently embrace U, V and W. I travelled back by tube once from a filming session at Ealing with Peter Ustinov. He asked if I had ever noticed how so many people getting into the tube look like someone famous; I said that up to now this thought had not occurred to me in my pilgrimages on either the District, Northern, Piccadilly or Circle lines. "You just watch at the next stop," said Peter. Clement Attlee got in; to be more exact, his absolute double. He was followed by Tessie O'Shea, and at the next stop by Lord Beaverbrook (except that he was wearing a cloth cap) and Hylda Baker. They were all identified promptly by Peter straight in their faces as they sat down or began strap-hanging. When at Sloane Square two very thin gentlemen with little moustaches and an equally thin lady without one joined us and Peter said, "Wilson, Keppel and Betty" I left him to continue his train-spotting and took a taxi to Victoria. V is slightly cheating, but all the Pullman cars on the Brighton Belle have ladies' names; my favourite car, mainly because the stewards warn me in advance if there is anyone dangerously talkative on the train, is called Vera. The most lethal of the Brighton Belle's journeys is the eleven p.m. from Victoria; this is the theatre train (a lot of theatre people live in Brighton) and you have to be very careful indeed if, after a long day's grind, you don't want to be trapped with a lot of gay chat about how fabulous the business was tonight, or how unreceptive the audience was all through Act One but how they brightened up after the interval. No doubt the other theatrical regulars have the same qualms about being trapped by me telling them how camera three packed up right in the middle of my most important close-up, but on these journeys I always buy the *Evening News* rather than the *Standard*. I have nothing against the *Standard*; it is an admirable newspaper and Clive is my favourite cartoon character. It is just that the *News* is bigger to hide behind. Not that this attempt at camouflage always works; Dora Bryan has an endearing habit of turning down the top of one's *Evening News*, saying, "Oh, it's you, dear," and sitting down and telling you about Daniel's mumps. Sir Laurence Olivier is a regular on this train. He was appearing in a play called *Semi-Detached* at the Saville a year or two ago before he became nationalised; for the part he had grown a rather sad, wispy moustache. Sir Laurence, if he will forgive my saying so, is unlikely to get into that list of the ten best-dressed men in the world; nor, come to that, am I. We both, unless forced to do otherwise, like to go casual. One night he only just managed to make the eleven o'clock Belle; he was carrying a battered little attaché case and this, combined with the moustache and an overcoat that had seen better days, was enough for the steward. "Second-class further back the train," he said, completely failing to recognise the late arrival. Sir Laurence went as directed. In a way it is rather typical of the man. And the W journey was the first time I went on an Emlyn Williams weekend. It was still war, and the late train on Saturday night was packed. We had to stand in the corridor; at least I stood and Emlyn sat on an upturned suitcase and never stopped scribbling on the backs of envelopes, bills, or anything he could lay his hands on. He even asked the airman standing next to him if he might borrow his evening paper and scribbled away on the vacant column of the stop press. When we got to his house, Mrs. Williams collected all the bits of paper and put them carefully away. They eventually formed part of a play called *The Wind of Heaven*. I wish I could do this: write anywhere, at any time, in any circumstances. I have to be at my own desk in my own house, with the typewriter in its correct position and the typing paper new and virgin white. At least the paper has to start off in that condition; often it remains in the same condition for some considerable time. But if I make a typing mistake or want to alter something three-quarters of the way down the sheet of foolscap, the sheet is ripped angrily out of the machine and I start all over again; I have to have a clean page in front of me. It is a great waste of time and paper. I have tried in the summer to work out in the garden; there is always a bee hovering or some irritating bird twittering or a snatch of conversation from the garden four houses away just too *sotto voce* to hear without a real effort; after half-an-hour I pack it in, go back to the assembly belt, strip to the waist and start typing and sweating. If only one could write as people like Emlyn Williams do: anywhere. If only one could have written such good plays.

X, Y, Z: the prospect of ending with Norman Vaughan playing the xylophone or Jimmy Young introducing Zero Mostel doing his coffee percolator routine is too frightening to contemplate. We can only thank Providence that in 'A to

Z' we dealt with our own alphabet and not the Cambodian one, which has seventy-four letters.

Shortly after 'A to Z' ended, my agent rang me one evening with the news that the well-known impresario, Mr. Harold Fielding, had lost his reason and wanted me to take over from Ian Carmichael in the leading part in *The Gazebo* which was running very successfully at the Savoy. When I was brought round with sal volatile and strong drink, I said. "Why me, for God's sake?" My agent, suggesting by his tone of voice that he, too, thought poor Mr. Fielding must be really very ill indeed, said he had no idea but would I do it? I said, "Yes, of course"; if I had said "no" I would have regretted it all my life, and I hadn't had a really good role since doing that 'Foolish Questions' monologue in my sailor suit in Wallace Green Church Hall in Berwick-upon-Tweed. Having said "Yes, of course," I went to the Savoy the following night and saw the play for the first time. It was quite a part, with the character hardly ever off the stage; and the fact that I had never appeared professionally on any stage in my life (apart from that matinée when I took over from the unfortunate young man in *Sky High*, and naturally I didn't get paid for that) seemed to me to confirm Mr. Fielding's mental blackout. Mr. Fielding, however, seemed blissfully happy about the whole thing and issued a statement to the Press saying that I would be the highest-paid actor in London. This, when I received my weekly stipend, proved to be inaccurate.

Moira Lister was the co-star, playing my wife. In recent years she has been my widow on T.V.; as well as wife and widow, we have enjoyed many other happy relationships over the past ten years or so. I rehearsed with the understudies; they were all very helpful indeed, but it was a little disheartening to be continually told "Mr. Carmichael always did it this way," or "Ian used to get a big laugh there." Miss Lister stayed well away, and with reason. I could imagine her thoughts on hearing who the replacement was to be; she and Ian were very good friends, and I am neither the same age, shape or star quality as Mr. Carmichael. And if (as no doubt she did) she had checked up and found that my previous stage experience had been 'Foolish Questions' in Berwick-upon-Tweed and that one matinée at the Phoenix, this cannot have filled her with any great confidence. She appeared at my last run-through of the play before opening; she sat with the director in the front row of the stalls, wearing an almost pure white fur coat and with that gorgeous mane of blonde hair almost shining in the darkness of the theatre. She never appeared to move a muscle while I battled on through the part; she just sat there with her arms folded and I decided that, no doubt with every justification, she hated both Mr. Fielding for thinking up the idea and me for saying "Yes". I was petrified of her; to me she was the epitome of glamour and sophistication, forever being photographed with the William Hickey gang at fashionable premières or dernières; always impeccably garbed and groomed, whereas I am given to slacks that should have gone years ago to the jumble and T-shirts with the remnants of last Tuesday's scrambled egg down the front. And hadn't she a house in Cadogan Square and was married to a French vicomte? She has since admitted in her own book—*The Very Merry Moira*, published, if I can get in another plug, by this same long-standing and un-healthy relationship between Mrs. Hodder and her friend, Miss Stoughton—that she was scared stiff of me. On my first night I was the one who was scared stiff and, at any rate at the beginning of the play, showed it. Just to make things easy for the new boy, the play opened with me alone on-stage loading a revolver, going up to draw some very wide and very heavy curtains—they had those two lengths of cord to open and close them and, of course, I got hold of the wrong cord—and then hiding behind a drinks cabinet and killing

Michael Goodliffe as dead as a doornail the moment he entered. I didn't, of course, really kill him, it was a cheat opening to the plot; you can't kill off as good an actor as Mr. Goodliffe the moment he comes on. But what with my hand shaking so much that I could hardly load the bullets in the revolver, grabbing hold of the wrong curtain cord, and the revolver failing to go off when I pulled the trigger and a stand-by shot having to be fired (rather late) from the wings, it was an inauspicious start to my West End career. *Career?* I have never been asked back; sometimes I wonder why.

I got through the first night somehow; the audience began by being either sceptical or curious and ended by being very kind indeed; if my elocution teacher in Berwick had been present I am sure she would again have said that I was a little trouper. The following afternoon a rehearsal was called, and it became obvious fairly soon that it was called for my benefit and for mine alone. After about the fiftieth request from the director that I should remain in a certain position and not meander towards the back of the set, I said to Moira, "You're not by any chance suggesting that I'm up-staging you, are you?" "Yes, dear," said Miss Lister. "And for someone who's never been on the stage before, you're far too bloody good at it. Now let's go across to the Savoy and have a great zonking drink." Since when I don't think we have ever stopped laughing. Although I had asked Mr. Fielding to let Moira move into it, I had inherited the star dressing-room; I needn't really have worried, because after two or three performances Moira moved in—not, of course, to change her smalls or put on her make-up—but to laugh. I had a splendid dresser called Mackie who prepared a dainty meal for us both between the shows on Saturday nights: very thinly-cut bread and butter (both brown and white), Tiptree's strawberry preserve, and extremely strong tea. I used to smuggle from Brighton in my brief-case some pâté and a half-bottle of Pouilly fumé and when Mackie left us we poured the contents of our tea-cups down the sink and I stuffed most of the bread and butter in my brief-case and we got down to the pâté and the Pouilly. Every night after the show Moira drove me to catch that same dangerous eleven o'clock Brighton Belle; we hardly ever left the theatre before seven minutes to eleven and the Vicomtesse's Jaguar was invariably facing the wrong way up Savoy Hill; she drove through lights of all colours and was apt to cry out "Cripple!" to any sluggish pedestrian trying to cross the Embankment. But I never missed the train once. I have to admit that on a number of occasions I had to vault the barrier. There was one night when the ticket-collector at the barrier said to me while I was in mid-vault, "You shouldn't do it, guv'nor. Not at your time of life."

Even with me taking over, the show ran for several more months at the Savoy; I then went out on tour with it. Once the labour pains were over I enjoyed every single moment of it; and there were a number of moments. The plot, if you could call it such, hinged on a body being buried under a gazebo which was built in the interval between the first and second acts; when the curtain rose on Act Two, there it was, seen through the windows on the top of a hill and in full view of the audience. One matinée it wasn't, the stage staff had omitted to set it. I was the first to notice its absence; with what seemed to me commendable presence of mind I pointed off-stage and talked about the gazebo that had been built in that field over there. Mr. Goodliffe then appeared on the scene, and, not having heard my placing of the wretched thing, pointed in quite the opposite direction and said didn't the gazebo look attractive across there on the top of that rising slope away to the south. Miss Lister then appeared, having heard neither of us, summed up the situation and said— pointing in yet another direction—"Doesn't the gazebo look absolutely right at the end of the drive?" The audience didn't seem to notice. Mr. Goodliffe didn't really like laughs, or at any rate not milking laughs: he was playing the part of a District Attorney and wanted to get on with solving the crime. At one performance, when I had to sit on the edge of a modern Scandinavian-type chair, the chair tipped over and I landed on my behind on the stage with the chair on top of me. I said to Moira, "I am fed up with all this modern furniture; what I wanted here was a *pouffe*." Miss Lister, it goes without saying, reacted at once. "A pouffe, dear?" she said. "Well, if you want a pouffe, you shall have a pouffe." "After all," I said, warming to the subject, "you can get pouffes anywhere. No difficulty in finding pouffes. Why, if I feel like having a pouffe, I cannot have a pouffe, I cannot imagine." After a few performances we worked this up into a nice little three-minute routine, with poor Michael standing by waiting to get back to his D.A. interrogation job. When we went on tour his part was taken over by Peter Gray; one Wednesday matinée in Wolverhampton—these things always seem to happen at a midweek matinée—an infant had been smuggled in, presumably in its mother's shopping-bag; it whimpered incessantly all through the first act. Peter and I had a long scene together on the sofa, nothing unhealthy, just discussing the crime; again, I don't know how I had the nerve, but I abandoned Peter on the settee, advanced to the footlights, did an Albert Finney or a Nicol Williamson, and said, "I'm sorry, ladies and gentlemen, but unless that baby is taken out, I'm afraid it's impossible to go on with the play." Peter is slightly deaf, not to any degree that ever affects his performance; when the act was over he said, "What was the line you slipped in halfway through the sofa scene? It's not in the script, is it?" He was the lucky one; he hadn't heard the baby.

It is wrong to preen, but every night I walked along the Strand to the Savoy Theatre and saw my name in lights at the corner of Savoy Court I am afraid I preened. I thought: it's taken a long time; I don't think the name deserves to be up there; thousands of actors and actresses who have been through drama school and repertory have never seen their names in lights and probably never will; and there is mine. One night all four l's in my name had fused. It looked very odd indeed, but I still preened.

8

THE CLICHÉ, successfully set to music, is that there is no business like show business. Often, of course, there is no business : period. Back go the kids to be part-time sales assistants at Moss Bros., or home helps or baby-sitters at five bob an hour. There is certainly no business in which the businessmen and women involved in it talk more shop; or on occasions, as has already been amply proved in this book, write more shop. A year or two ago I was at a non-theatrical party in Brighton; at least it was almost wholly clean and civilian, but there was a sprinkling of us and—as always happens—within minutes we were huddled together in a tight little coterie in one corner of the room and were off about the notices for Margaret Leighton's play and was it true that *Up Your Jumper* was coming off and had you heard what the Master said when he met Henry Sherek halfway up a Swiss Alp and how in God's name did Mavis think she'd get away with that part at her time of life. A distinguished don at Sussex University who had been hovering on the fringe of the coterie entered the conversational lists for the first time. "It's been extraordinarily interesting," he said. "I've been listening to you ladies and gentlemen for almost half-an-hour, and you might have been talking Urdu; I haven't understood a single word you've said. In fact, had you been talking Urdu, I would have been more enlightened. I know a little Urdu." As he moved off in search of more rational conversation, one of the shoptalkers in our group said, "I feel sorry for that poor little Urdu he knows; he's got a nasty, sleazy glint in his eye, that old man has."

Much the same thing happened one night on the Brighton Belle. I was coming back from London; someone else in the business joined me (you will notice that people in the entertainment world refer to it simply as "the business," implying that there are no other businesses that matter); once again we were off. Sitting at the table opposite was an elderly, pinstriped, distinguished-looking gentleman reading, or trying to read, the financial columns of the evening papers. Again around Gatwick, he lowered his newspaper, took off his reading glasses, turned to us and asked if we would do him the honour of joining him in a modicum of liquid refreshment. We were a little taken aback, but readily agreed to do him the honour. When the drinks arrived and we had raised our glasses to our unknown benefactor, he said, "I wish to make it clear that these drinks are proffered through no sudden philanthropic impulse. It's simply that since the train left Victoria you two have never drawn breath, and I have not understood a single bloody word you've said. I am in steel. I propose to devote the remainder of this journey in explaining to you two gentlemen the disastrous results of the nationalisation of steel, the possible economic consequences of denationalising it, and the future—if any—of the steel industry as a whole." He did, too; the pair of us never uttered another word. He rounded off his peroration neatly as the train slid into Brighton Station, rose, collected his bowler and briefcase, said with Churchillian panache, "Good-day to you, gentlemen," and left. I admired him; there are times when I wish I had the courage to stop even my own set in mid-shop. It is for the most part such a very small shop, by no means a multiple store.

Some of us, however, manage to have a few other interests to talk about apart from shop. Mine mainly concern the town I live in and which I adore. I used to keep a pied-à-terre in

London where I could stay if I was working late at night; I used it so seldom that I gave it up. I would rather catch the midnight train (no Pullman cars, no drinks, no Dora) or the milk-train; smell the clean, fresh air even when walking down the platform at Brighton, and be home. Home for me is a tall house with far too many stairs in what is loosely described as a typically Regency terrace; actually it is nothing of the sort. It is Victorian and was built in 1851; Brighton estate agents describe almost everything as Regency, very little is. It stands high on a hill overlooking the town and the sea; we have all, through years of what Stephen Potter would have called next-door-neighbourmanship, persuaded or shamed each other into painting the fronts of our houses (in some cases even the backs) pure white; when the sun shines the whole terrace gleams so brightly that it is almost sore on the eyes. It is in a part of Brighton happily removed from the day trippers or the night-life racket; it is a village. The little shop around the corner will cash you a cheque if you run short; when Gilbert Harding also lived round the corner there was a fairly permanent drain on the till and one had to be there very early in the morning. Now my only real cheque-cashing competitor is Hector Bolitho, who lives round the other corner and is, in my view, unfair about cashing cheques. He employs a runner. It isn't a large house, but it is a *home*; it's warm and comfortable, and I know that when my friends come in for drinks in the evening one always sits in that armchair and one always in that one, and they know that I always sit in my own one in the corner with the light behind me to minimise the bags under my eyes. It has a small terraced garden, so sheltered in the summer when the trees are in full leaf that you can sun-bathe stark naked without the neighbours being either erotically stirred or what the Scots call scunnered. At least, I hope this is so; I have seen certain flutterings of lace curtains on either side when I lie out and expose the lot in mid-August. At the top of the garden is a mini-greenhouse in which for a time I grew orchids; it proved an expensive pastime. The heat required for rearing any really exotic orchid is so high that the quarterly electricity bills were exorbitant; worse, the greenhouse was so hot that everything else wilted and died, including almost on one occasion myself. Now I specialise mainly in begonias. The most famous begonia-breeding firm in the world are Blackmore and Langdon of Bath (commercial plug: just two dozen corms at the start of the next potting season, if you don't mind); each season they introduce usually three new varieties, after a great deal of inter-breeding and sexual activities in their begonia beds. Begonia sex is unlike ours; the male is a puny, you would think impotent little nonentity; the female, once she gets the urge, ends up looking like Diana Dors. Three years ago Messrs. Blackmore and Langdon said they would like to name one of their new varieties after me. I was extremely flattered; they even sent me free samples of myself. Mr. Langdon said in an explanatory letter that the three new varieties they were introducing that year were a pale lemon with delicate cream tinges, a single pure white with picotee edges, and a very large, hardy, florid deep crimson. The first two, he thought, didn't really suit me; the third, he felt, was definitely me. I cannot think why. But it is very satisfying to take someone into the greenhouse, point at the large, hardy, florid deep crimson job, and say "Me, dear." The only trouble is that last year I contracted some disease through over-watering myself and kept falling off. The other unfortunate thing is that I started off in the catalogue at three guineas and am now down to £1 10s. od. That, again, is show business.

I am lucky in my location in Brighton. There is what is known as the smart end away along to the east, where Sir Laurence and Lady Olivier, Sir John and Lady Clements, Dame Flora Robson, Dora Bryan, and all the really classy people live. There is the Hove end where Elizabeth Allen and Robert Coote live and where Phyllis Dare goes down to the front heavily veiled in case someone recognises her and offers her a job. "Silly bitch," says her sister Zena, who in her unbelievable eighties is furious if she's not working. Between these two extremes, there I am; and very pleasant it is, too. It is pleasant to be able to invite either the left or the right flank in for drinks; pleasant to be left alone and be part of the village. I have good neighbours; my local, which is presided over by a lady called Nasty (because she is so nice) is more a club than a pub; the vicar calls me "darling"; Mr. Rose, the newsagent, says it couldn't matter less when I come out without any money early in the morning in my bedroom slippers and am screaming for twenty Senior Service; the Irishman in the off-licence round the corner says "Not you again, for Chroist's sake; Holy Mother o' God, you had a bottle only two noights ago"; and Mrs. Mair in Number 12, whom I had always regarded as eminently respectable and therefore to be avoided, said to me when we eventually spoke at a party at Denise Robbins', "You know I played Eliza in *Pygmalion* at Birmingham Rep., when Maggie Leighton was a student." David Heneker lives at Number 22 and churns out the scores for *Half a Sixpence* and other shows in a sound-proof studio in his back garden. I type away in the attic room at the top of my house, and it is plain from the expression on some of the neighbours' faces that they devoutly wish that that, too, was sound-proofed. In the gardens opposite, which belong to us, Mr. Mair burns all our rubbish in a series of spectacular bonfires, carefully choosing the day when the wind is just right to carry the smoke in the direction of anyone he has taken a slight turn against; the University students who have digs near where I live lie out in the same gardens and get up to the lot, seriously disrupting my output. The kids in Number 4 cycle or tricycle or scooter at break-neck speed along the terrace, more or less stark naked in summer; they narrowly avoid head-on collisions with my godson

Rufus, who lives round yet another corner and scooters in the opposite direction. In disentangling them one morning, I asked Rufus how old he was; I had an ominous feeling that he had a birthday coming up. "Four," he said. "How old are you?" "I am a hundred and two," I told him. I had just done *The Vortex* with Margaret Leighton on B.B.C. T.V.; we had both caught an unhappy glimpse of ourselves on the colour monitor, which reveals all. I said, "God, I look a hundred and two." Miss Leighton said, "You're lucky, dear: I look two hundred and two." Rufus was unimpressed by the figure. "Only a hundred and *two*?" he said. "The lady next door to us is *much* older than that." It is that sort of terrace; it is fun.

I play tennis, always with the same foursome, and bridge usually with the same quartet. My regular tennis partner in men's doubles is some thirty years younger than I; I find myself nowadays saying, "Can you?" more frequently than in earlier years, and there are moments when he says, "Frankly, with you in that position, *no*." Apart from anno domini, this may be just possibly due to an incident which happened many years ago when I was hi-jacked into being a line judge in a final involving Drobny. Drobny did one of his impeccable little drop-shots on to the tramlines; I said, quite firmly, "Out"; and Drob, with great charm, looked at me and said, "You need specs." He was perfectly right; I had my eyes tested the following week and have worn them ever since. In reverse, one of my regular bridge partners whose eyesight is somewhat failing called two spades one evening and—encouraged by me, I had a great many spades, starting off with the K, J, 10—ended up in a grand slam in spades, doubled by the opposition and confidently re-doubled by the lady who until then had been my friend. She took a Kleenex tissue out of her handbag, demisted her glasses, and said, "Oh dear, I knew it was a black suit I had a lot of. They're clubs."

I swim, always on the same beach. It is an oddity of the Island Race that they love to be cheek-by-jowl. In Brighton they swarm down from the station, park themselves, their children, their picnic-baskets and their transistors at the most two feet away from their neighbours on the *plage* and enjoy it. Half a mile on either side of them there are empty and better and cleaner beaches. I patronise one known as Medina *plage*; I went in one summer evening for a late-night swim; the tide was out and you had to wade for an eternity until the sea even reached your navel. I was flopping about when an angler on the end of the groin at one side of Medina *plage* appeared to have gone berserk. He kept jumping up and down and flaying his arms and I then heard the word, "Sharks!" Johnny Weismuller couldn't have made the pebbles faster. I ran along to the end of the groin and there they were; two, to me, enormous sharks gambolling. It was explained to me by some expert on the subject that they were basking sharks who came close in-shore in the hot weather and that they were perfectly harmless, but I am not one to do my plodding breast-stroke in between a couple of sharks, however basking. I have enough sharks to contend with in the theatre.

My local, the Neptune, which as I said is more a club than a pub, is in actual fact more Crufts than either. Daisy, an outsize black Labrador owned by—or, to be strictly accurate, owning—Elizabeth Allen and her husband, Bill O'Bryen, asks for a tomato juice so fervently that if you are wearing a cardigan or a sweater the knitting is unpurled. She prefers her tomato juice without Worcester sauce, just neat. Rudi, the dachshund who runs the ménage, has a habit of lying upside-down in his basket with a Watney's beer-mat which someone has skilfully thrown covering his balls; there is a fox-terrier of uncertain age whose master—or, again, servant—describes as the oldest tart in Hove, which is saying something. In the summer months a great gang of delightful youngsters storms into the pub straight off the beach, wearing only the briefest of briefs; William Kendall and Robert Coote pop in, have their drinks, and cash cheques; once I took Moira Lister to the hostelry and a complete stranger came up to her and said, "I'll never forget you in *Red Shoes*, dear: you were fabulous." "Thank you," said Miss Lister somewhat tartly. "That was Moira Shearer." It was the Neptune which, when I first came to live in Brighton, decided my church-going habits. I am what I suppose you would call low C. of E. I like to join in; if there is a pop on the hymn list like 'O Worship the King All Glorious Above' or 'While Shepherds Watched their Flocks by Night' I belt it out to such a degree that people eight pews in front of me look round to see what is going on. I like a good, short sermon, one that sends me out thinking, even if I may not agree with everything that has been said in it; I like a vicar who knows how important it is to pronounce the benediction dead on opening time on a Sunday morning. I am anti-incense and irked by incomprehensible intoning; when I first came to Brighton I had difficulty in finding a church which fitted. It is like finding a tailor; some do the jacket all right and can't do the trousers; or, worse, they put the blame for their ill-fitting trousers on the customers' own behinds. On one of my earliest visits to the Neptune a tall, distinguished, silver-haired cleric came into the bar, said "5 and 2, please," had his drink poured out, put it down in one, said with great courtesy, "Thank you, dear lady: I give you good-day," and left. I was intrigued. The next time I patronised the establishment the same thing happened, except that on this occasion the clerical character said, "3 and 1." By this time I had got on speaking terms with Nasty; I asked her what this mysterious code was. She explained that the padre always drank gin and French; that the order was phrased to indicate the ratio of gin to Noilly Prat; she was unkind enough to hint that it largely depended on how the collection had gone, and that sometimes it was as high as

5 to 1 and sometimes down to evens. I said he sounded exactly the sort of vicar I was after; she told me where his church was, adding that I had better be there early because of the queue. Although I am a believer, this naturally I disbelieved; you don't nowadays have queues outside churches, except perhaps little ones on Easter Sunday or Christmas Day. She was perfectly right; you had to queue to get in and often extra chairs had to be placed down the aisle. All because of the man's personality; he was the best preacher I have ever listened to and knew all about winding up proceedings dead on time. Well, of course; he was in the Neptune himself four minutes after the benediction, asking for either "3 and 2" or "4 and 1" depending on how things had gone. He was, I am sure, a much less saintly man than many vicars who preach Sunday after Sunday to almost non-existent congregations; he may indeed have been a bit of a rascal; but he could fill his church. We became great friends; I was a member of his Parochial Church Council and I used to read the lessons for him; he came to my house often and I remember one night when he left he said to me, "You know, we've a great deal in common, you and I: the one thing that matters is being able to *put it across*." He, too, was perfectly right; he had, of course, the greatest thing in the world to put across; all that I have is triviality. But whether it be fundamental or froth, unless you can put it over to the customers it is a waste of their time and yours.

I enjoy cooking; I rather fancy myself as a cook. I make a great deal of mess in the kitchen and it is a golden rule that no-one is allowed in while I am over the hot stove. To my credit, or I think it is to my credit, I also enjoy washing-up; you can think beautiful thoughts while gently swilling plates in Fairy Liquid or you can vent your spleen on someone you have taken a turn against while scratching away with the Brillo at some maddening saucepan that has become encrusted with the remains of scrambled eggs, or worse. And there is an immense satisfaction, after the holocaust which I create in my kitchen, in seeing everything clean and shining and put away in their proper places. I never weigh; the ingredients are just plunged in; usually it works. It is like being green-fingered at gardening. When preparing, for instance, a casserole or a coq au vin I like to keep adding things and tasting; bouquet garni or a further sprinkling of sage or thyme, a couple of left-over leeks I have found in the larder, another slosh of Macon or maybe just a little more brandy; by the time the dish has been simmering for an hour or so and I have been steadily sampling it there really isn't enough left for the number of guests I have invited to dinner and I am more or less plastered. Weights and measures in cookery books seem to me in any case meaningless. I have quite a library of cookery books in my kitchen, ranging from Mrs. Beeton through Larousse to something called *Le Veritable Cuisine de Provence*; they all say things like "add two teacupfuls of water and simmer gently." "What size of teacup, for God's sake?" I ask—usually out loud, all by myself with my apron on and my glasses steamed up. I have at least seven different sizes and varieties of teacups, from the very dainty little Crown Derby numbers, which are only brought out when either the vicar or Godfrey Winn comes to tea, to enormous containers which look more like babies' potties and hold just under a pint. The one thing that really defeats me in the Escoffier racket is dumplings. I have tried making dumplings in every known way and in several ways unknown even to Fanny Cradock; with ordinary suet, with Atora and the rest of them, boiling them slowly, swiftly, and at medium temperatures; they just take one look at me and end up as porridge and very poor porridge at that.

Johnson said that when a man is tired of London he is tired of life; but then Samuel didn't live in the allegedly swinging London of the nineteen-seventies. Shelley was perhaps nearer the mark when he wrote, "Hell is a city much like

London"; though, to be fair, neither did Percy Bysshe know the London of today. I still love London, but I find—after a day or a night, or maybe both, working in it—I want to get the hell out of it, back home. As has been made all too clear, my home life is ordinary and humdrum: the house, the garden, playing tennis or bridge, swimming, cooking, bashing a typewriter, having the neighbours in for drinks or going for drinks to the neighbours, getting worked up when one of Mr. Mair's bonfires seems to be heading in my direction or when my godson falls off his scooter and yells the terrace down. It is in a way heartening to find—when one is thinking what far more exciting and glamorous lives people like the Oliviers and Anna Neagle or Dora Bryan must lead along at the smart end of the town—that they, too, when they are at home lead ordinary lives. Now let us get back to business. The business. In the foolish view of those of us in it, the only business.

By early in the sixties I was becoming more and more hooked on television and gradually less and less enchanted with the theatre. Perhaps the theatre had become disenchanted with me; if that was so, the mood was mutual. Television is a frightening but fascinating medium to work in; but if you bring something off on it, it is very satisfying indeed to know that several millions of people have either seen you appear or watched something you have written. Preening again, no doubt, but I get a little inward glow when a taxi-driver recognises me and says, 'Saw you on the box last night, guv'nor"—even if he adds "funny: I always thought you was a bit more sawn-off, like," or simply, "the missus didn't think much of it; nothing to it, she said; just a load of old crap, the missus thought it was." There is an immediacy about working in television, especially in a regular weekly series, which I find exciting and stimulating. It is, of course, hard work. In the various series I have been involved in over the past two or three years—shows like 'The Very Merry Widow,' 'Misleading Cases,' and 'Before the Fringe'—the mummers normally parade on Monday at ten a.m. on the dot in some church hall or boys' club in some un-get-at-able part of London with some ridiculous postal address like N.W.69. They rehearse all week; when they are not actually at the words they are tearing for fittings or sessions at Wig Creations or filming on location for some sequence in the following week's show which can't be done live in the studio. If, as usually happens, they are putting the show in the can on the Sunday, they have to be on the studio floor again at ten in the morning; they are there in make-up and costume under those blazing hot lights until the studio audience starts to queue up and they know that in less than an hour they will be at it. Acting on television has all the nervous tension of acting in the theatre or in films; more. Every night is a first night; you haven't even the satisfaction of knowing that, if you get away with it first time, you can go on churning out the same routine—and be paid for the churning—for as long as the clientèle keep coming in. You have to learn what is often a very long part and do it, or hope and pray to do it, in what amounts to a single take, unlike filming, where you may spend a whole day on one or two lines until they are to the director's satisfaction. And usually in situation comedy—which is what I mainly dabble in— you have to play to a small studio audience, perhaps no more than three or four hundred people; try to keep them happy while bearing in mind that the audience you are really play-ing to are those millions sitting in their front parlours. Some-times, I know, the end products are fairly dismal, but the efficiency of television excites me. When you arrive at ten a.m. on that first Monday, the floor of the church hall or boys' club in N.W.69 is already marked out with tape so that you know to an inch just how far the door that is going to be over there is from the table that will be set down there;

by the Thursday the heads of the technical departments—the camera crews, the lighting and sound technicians—are watching you and finding out precisely where an actor is going to be (if he remembers) on such-and-such a line in shot 287. I was in a play of mine in repertory a few months ago; even at the end of the third week of rehearsal the director was still saying, "Duckies, shall we try playing that scene to the right of the sofa instead of the left?" and when you pointed out that if you went right of the sofa you would collide with the drinks table, he would say, "Shall we be absolute devils, duckies, and move the drinks table?" I may have been lucky with the directors I have worked for on T.V.; I think I have been. But everything is planned; it has to be—there is no time for dithering. And from the writer's point of view, life is infinitely more satisfactory than in what is for some reason still called the live theatre. In offering you a job on television or in accepting a script, they mean what they say; if they give you a transmission date, you know that—barring some unforeseen disaster—the show will go out on that date; when they offer you a fee, you know it will be paid and paid on the dot. I am speaking mainly of the B.B.C., because I work for them much more than for commercial television; but on the occasions I have worked for the other lot, I have found them equally efficient and good to deal with. I wish I could say the same of the commercial theatre at the present time; its main trouble is, I am sure, because for the first time in their lives people have got complete entertainment in their own homes for what amounts to a few shillings a week as opposed to the cost of a night out at the theatre; but part of the malaise is, I suspect, due to managerial inefficiency which almost amounts to dishonesty. I shook a rather clammy handshake on August 15th, 1968, with a very famous impresario; he had professed the greatest enthusiasm over a musical I had just finished; we had got down to discussing cast and director and choreographer and so on. My agents, Mr. and Mrs. Eric

Glass (they are known as the Glass Menagerie) were with me at the session; the impresario told Eric that he wanted the contract drawn up and sent to him as quickly as possible. This was done within three days. On August 15th, 1969, absolutely nothing having transpired, the contract unsigned, not a penny of option money forthcoming, I told the Glass Menagerie that I was going to send the impresario an anniversary telegram. The Glass Menagerie hinted that this might be unwise. I nearly sent one on August 15th, 1970, but by then I had lost interest. I wouldn't really mind if a theatre management turned a show down flat; but to accept it, appear wildly enthusiastic, and then do nothing about it irritates me. The managements, of course, have many perfectly valid excuses for delay; they can't get the stars they want, no suitable theatre is available, they've just lost a packet in some other production, and so on. But there is an increasing tendency among the West End managements today to sit on a property for as long as possible without even paying out the miserly advance for a six-month option, renewable for another six months. For a straight play this usually amounts to two hundred pounds; the play may have taken six months to write, a further six months to be read and "accepted," and at least a year to be "got off the ground" before anything happens in the way of signing that cheque for two hundred pounds. The advance is, in any case, on account of royalties earned when, if ever, the show is put on; the management, unless the show is an immediate disaster, doesn't stand to lose very much so far as the author's whack is concerned. This is the currently fashionable phrase: "getting it off the ground"; managements are loth to commit themselves until all the pieces in the jig-saw—cast, theatre, director, designer, and so on—have fitted into place. Meanwhile the wretched author remains unpaid for his wares; few of us have the nerve to tell a management to go to hell and can we have our scripts back, but spread over a period of two years the option money, if my mathematics are right, works out at under two pounds a week. I am lucky; I can just say "Nuts" and go on (I hope) writing for television or doing the occasional acting job. But the delaying of payment for something that has been accepted until everything has been "got off the ground" seems to me an unethical procedure; it is like having a ton of coal delivered in the early spring and telling the coal merchant, "I'm keeping it, of course, but I'm not paying you until we start lighting a fire in the late autumn." Except that in the theatre it is very often the late autumn three years later, if ever. I may be very old-fashioned, but to me a deal is a deal and a handshake, however clammy, ought to mean something. And they never—theatre managements, I mean—return scripts. They just lose them.

All this sounds like an outsize bunch of sour grapes. People are forever asking me why in the past few years I have concentrated on television and done so little in the theatre. Some of the answers have just been given; there are no doubt others. In the back of my mind is the nagging thought that it might just possibly be that I have become out of touch with the contemporary theatre; that the only sort of play I can write —which still has French windows, staircases, plots with beginnings, middles and ends, and in which no-one appears in the nude unless it is absolutely necessary—are now old-hat. I brush this nag away as completely unworthy. I have, in fact, written quite a lot for the theatre in the past few years, little or nothing of which has yet been seen in this country. At the time of writing I have two big-scale musicals and two straight plays on the shelves, all of them accepted (some several times over by different managements) and none of which has yet "got off the ground." One of the plays—a comedy called *Finder Please Return*—began its career in, of all places, Baden-Baden, and has since been produced in Paris (starring that delectable Dany Robin), Athens, Madrid, Berlin and Hamburg. It is the usual frothy nonsense, and the

Continent seems hopelessly behind this country in being content with frothy nonsense as long as it is well done. Perhaps if ever we manage to get into the Common Market we can exert our influence on the Six and make them realise how behind the times they are still to appreciate an evening when all an audience is called upon to do is laugh; no messages, no four-letter words, no transvestism or violence, no battering babies to death in their carry-cots, no confused thinking that it is dramatically with-it to do things on the stage which are done better in the privacy of one's own home. Just a good, solid night's entertainment. How square can you get?

My contributions to the theatre in this country during the sixties included at least three memorable occasions. When I say memorable, the few who saw them will have forgotten them within hours if they had any sense, but they are memorable to me. I had a play of mine tried out at the Playhouse, Newcastle; no-one had checked up in advance to find that the theatre was already in compulsory liquidation and that in any case—even without assistance from me—it was due to close after the run of the piece. It was not what one would call a financially rewarding engagement. I had a comedy called *Everything Happens on a Friday* out on what was optimistically described as a prior-to-London tour. This was disaster. Everything happened, not only on the Friday, but on the Monday, Tuesday, Wednesday, Thursday and at both performances on the Saturday. Except at the box-office; very little happened there. The leading lady, who must remain anonymous (but was in fact Irene Handl) was herself going through a writing phase; she was writing a very strange novel called *The Sioux*. If she had confined her writing to *The Sioux* I wouldn't have minded in the least; but she also re-wrote not only her own part but pretty well everyone else's. I was doing a T.V. series at the time and couldn't keep as beady an eye on the proceedings as I should have done; the director and Miss Handl failed to hit it off and the director had to go in mid-tour; the management had presented Miss Handl in a previous play which had been a big success and were anxious not to have an up-and-downer with the lady; and in any case I was—and still am—a great admirer of Irene's and thought, perhaps weakly, that this was the way she worked and that all would come right in the end. It didn't. We emptied theatres up and down the country and by the ninth and last week of the tour the morale of the company was at rock-bottom. We were playing the King's, Southsea; I drove over to see the Monday night performance in the company of some forty-odd patrons, few if any of whom I suspect had paid. We had no West End theatre and no further touring dates booked; the management still clung to the hope that some miracle comparable again to the dividing of the Red Sea would happen; perhaps the B.B.C. would offer us a television excerpt which would prove such a riot that the box-office would be kept working overtime for years. This seemed to me unlikely, and I decided that someone had to show some signs of efficiency and action; I came home and wrote two very long and strongly-worded letters. One was to Miss Handl saying exactly what I thought of the management; the other to the management telling them precisely what I thought of Miss Handl. By a genuine mistake (I swear it on my oath) I put the letters in the wrong envelopes. It certainly resulted in action; the show folded that Saturday in Southsea.

And at the very end of the decade some misguided management decided to send Cicely Courtneidge and Jack Hulbert out on tour in a revival of *Dear Charles*. I didn't want it to happen; I still had those memories of Yvonne and I knew that Cis was wrong for the part. But it is difficult to say, "No! you can't do it," especially when dealing with good friends; it was even harder to stop the show coming to London when it had been playing to excellent business in the provinces. Again we had director trouble; on this occasion the director and Jack didn't see eye to eye; the director once more departed in mid-tour and I took over myself. The two stars and the rest of the company worked like Trojans; I have never understood why Trojans have this reputation for hard work, the main thing they seem to have done was to haul that wooden horse into their city, and look where that got them. But the Hulberts, bless them, would gladly rehearse all day, do the show at night, and be ready to sit up until three in the morning discussing it. I was exhausted, and I knew that all the work was going to be in vain. The play was brought into the Duke of York's, only a hundred yards or so down St. Martin's Lane from the theatre where it had run for nearly two years; it had a pathetic little stay of three weeks. I think one of the saddest moments I have known was to visit first Cis's dressing-room and then Jack's between the second and third acts on their last Saturday night. They had both started packing; putting away the clothes they had worn in the first two acts and wouldn't be needing again. They had brought a lot of their personal belongings to the theatre, hoping (as actors always do) that they would be installed in their rather poky little dressing-rooms for a long time; that the rooms would become their second home. Framed photographs of each other and of members of their family; drinks and glasses to entertain anyone who might be popping round on the two hundredth performance; these, as well as the usual flowers in vases round the rooms and the first-night telegrams pinned up on the walls. Cis was already starting to stow away the vases and unpin the telegrams. Last nights are always miserable occasions, especially when they more or less coincide with the first night. It is worse when the circumstances involve two great stars who have served the theatre and the public so well for so long. I must say, like Dora Bryan after my crucifixion of her in Manchester, they both bounced back with remarkable resilience and were off on tour again and packing them in with Agatha Christie in no time.

But, so far as I was concerned, the theatrical score in the second half of the sixties totted up to an unprofitable try-out in Newcastle, a disaster on tour, and a revival which should never have been allowed near London. Thank God, I thought, for P. Nipkow. You may not have heard of the gentlemen, but—according to the *Encyclopedia Britannica* —he was the guy who in 1884 thought up a sort of scanning disc device with a great many holes in it; and this in the fullness of time led to television.

But if for me the theatre during most of the sixties was a sad succession of flops, television was non-stop and all go. When Southern Television opened up I was asked to script and appear in their gala opening night programme; no expense was spared except perhaps, I thought, in the scripting fee. Line Renaud was brought over from Paris; she still sends me Christmas cards reminding me of the sketch we did together about a Frenchwoman being given directions on how to locate the Southampton studios "... première à gauche après le gas-works, la deuxième à droit après la toilette publique et après ça encore la deuxième à droit après le dump pour anciennes voitures." Gracie was imported from Capri, sang 'Volare' both in the programme itself and several times during the bun-fight which followed, at the end of which she wrapped up all the left-over vol-au-vents in a serviette and took them home for herself and Boris. I did another sketch with Diana Dors, who at that time was allegedly farming in Sussex; what is more, poor soul, we sang a duet. It started off :

A.M.   How ya gonna keep 'em down on the farm
       After they've seen D.D.? . . .
D.D.   How ya gonna keep 'em safely from harm
       Once they start diggin' me? . . .

and continued in this witty and sophisticated vein. There was a large orchestra conducted by Eric Winstone and an equally large ladies' choir dressed in pale blue satin; Clive Lythgoe played the piano; Joyce and Lionel Blair danced more or less all over the *Queen Elizabeth* which was handily in Southampton docks; the audience, crammed into what little space was left in the studio, seemed to consist entirely of chains: every Mayor and Mayoress, Lord Mayor and Lady Mayoress for miles around had been invited. By the number of empty bottles at the end of the bun-fight, Southern was well launched.

Following the launching I did twenty-six late-night shows for Southern, once again called 'Melvillainy.' Just myself on a stool, with Charles Zwar at the piano and tymps and a double bass. The shows were satirical send-ups of the week's news; it was years before 'That Was the Week, That Was.' No prompt or autocue, you had to learn the beastly stuff, and if something cropped up in the nine o'clock news on a Saturday night which seemed ripe for comment I wrote a lyric during the supper-break and Charles wrote the tune and we shoved the new item in when we went on the air at eleven. We were supposed to run half-an-hour, but as we were the closing programme it didn't really matter if we overran by ten minutes or so. It was fun to be given a completely free hand to cotton on to any item in the week's news—grave, gay, important, unimportant—and say what you liked about it. One week the vicar of the Anglican Church in Monaco had admitted in the Press that he had to be cautious about including anything in his service at Matins that might send his flock straight to the casino divinely inspired. I did a piece about the beauty of the twenty-third psalm when well read, especially if one went straight from Matins, backed rouge and vingt-trois, and they both came up. Or the possible risks, if the first lesson was from Exodus, in even mentioning Joseph the son of Nun and the entire congregation backing zero. Never, of course, to preach a sermon on any text like "Mind not high things" (Romans : xi : 16) which would automatically induce the worshippers to back the low numbers as soon as the service was over and the casino had opened. In fact, if you wanted to retain the attention of your congregation, to skip the Book of Numbers altogether. It could set them off thinking of other things : systems, and whether the fact that sept had come up thirteen times running directly after Evensong last Sunday, when the vicar had been going on about remembering the seventh day and keep it holy, had any real religious significance.

If send-uppable news was in short supply, I just inserted lyrics about anything that took my fancy. One Saturday I had just played for the several hundredth time a scratchy old record of Bea Lillie doing her inimitable 'Fairies at the Bottom of my Garden.' (She did it later in 'Before the Fringe'; she has been doing it for generations, but she was tired and nervous, she dried completely halfway through the number and said to her accompanist, "What number are we supposed to be doing, dear?" When he said, "Fairies, Miss Lillie," she said, "Oh, I thought we were doing 'Maud'.") Short of material for that Saturday I thought of the condition of my own garden's bottom; at least the result filled up three minutes programme time . . .

> There are positively,
> Definitely,
> And quite understandably,
> *No* fairies at the bottom of my garden.
>
> I've concealed myself for hours
> In some horrid cauliflowers
> In the hope that I'd eventually spot 'em;
> But each fairy and each elf
> Says quite firmly to itself
> "I shall *not* go near that ghastly garden's bottom."

Not a banshee, troll, or dryad,
Nor a leprechaun or naiad
(It doesn't really matter how you name them)
Has ever left its card in
The bottom of my garden
And, being frank, you really cannot blame them.

There's a sordid heap of vegetable matter
Which gives off a strong and unattractive smell.
There are empty tins galore,
Broken bottles by the score,
But you never catch a glimpse of Tinkerbell.
No elfin feet will ever pitter-patter
Around my garden's bottom, I am sure;
And you cannot blame a gnome
For rejecting as its home
A place whose leading feature is manure.
There's a cesspool filled with green and stagnant water;
There's a broken fence with miles of rusty wire;
There are forty million flies
And one can't express surprise
That it's not a spot the little folk admire.
Although at times I've seen the gardener's daughter
Go down there—on occasions with a friend—
I have never noticed Puck
Weaving spells through all the muck
Which amasses at my garden's nether end.
There's an ancient pair of boots, and lots of nettles;
It is dismal, dreary, dirty, dank and drab;
It is not the sort of thing
Where you find a fairy ring
Or expect to meet Titania or Mab.
There are several old and battered pots and kettles;
There's a stack of rotting rhubarb leaves as well;
Not a fairy's ever tried it

For, quite rightly, they've decided
That the bottom of my garden's bloody hell.

And that is why there are absolutely
Irrefutably,
And quite justifiably
No fairies at the bottom of my garden.

A lady in Chichester, after hearing this epic, wrote in to inform me quite seriously that if I really had a cesspool filled with green and stagnant water at the bottom of my garden, there was a very good firm in Portsmouth which specialised in draining cesspools. The half-year of those late-night shows on Southern were fun to do; I don't think many people sat up to watch them, but we had a ball at our end.

I think I enjoy writing lyrics more than writing anything else. It is a thing you either can or cannot do, you can't be taught how to do it. (I don't think, after the kindergarten stage, you can be taught how to write.) Lyrics are not poetry, certainly not in my case; they could be called verse in that they rhyme here and there, but it is verse written to be sung or spoken rather than read. When I re-read a lyric of mine, the main enjoyment I get out of it is hearing again how it was originally put across by whatever star put it across. Like a revue sketch, a lyric must have a solid basic idea; often it is a twist on some well-known and accepted precept, like the contrast between my own garden's bottom and the bottoms of other people's gardens, all redolent with fairies. There was an excellent lyric in *Sweet and Low*—not written by me—called 'Borgia Orgy'; it was simply four members of the Borgia family anticipating with relish the dinner-party they were throwing that evening. It began, as good lyrics should do, by stating the premise :

The Borgias are having an orgy;
There's a Borgia orgy tonight.
But isn't it sickening—
We've run out of strychnine:
The gravy will have to have ground glass for thickening.

I can still see the happy glint of anticipation in Miss Gingold's eye when, after the lines:

When the butler flings open the dining-room door
There's a cunning contraption concealed in the floor:

she had to add, to round off the first chorus:

We wonder who'll sit on the circular saw
At the Borgia orgy tonight.

The greatest lyric-writers of the past half-century are Coward and Farjeon. In his revue *Sigh No More*, Coward wrote a brilliant lyric called 'Nina'; it was about a lady from Argentina who was mad about dancing the samba and fell in love with a sailor with a wooden leg. As well as being very funny, it was filled to capacity with double and triple rhymes; it had such a verbal rhythm to it that it hardly needed music; I envied it. We were just about to do the third of the Ambassadors revues; there had been a great deal of chat about the Master's wartime activities; he was alleged, while touring all over the place for E.N.S.A., to be doing highly important work for the Government, or just plain, common-or-garden spying; the subject seemed yelling out to be dealt with in lyric form and I was determined to attempt the same sort of rhyming and rhythm that Noël had done in his own revue. The number was written for Henry Kendall; in the end, I need hardly say, it was performed—brilliantly, again, I have to admit—by Hermione Gingold. It was called simply 'Noël, Noël' ...

When Europe was attacked and overpowered,
Mr. Coward,
Though ostensibly performing just for E.N.S.A.
Was asked by Mr. Churchill to commence a
Diplomatic tour to save the British Raj.
Through his efforts, Fascist plots in West Australia
Proved quite a failure
And while entertaining troops in Kuala Lumpur
He shoved several secret papers up his jumper
And escaped to Indo-China on a barge.
Humming tunes from *Bitter Sweet*, he
Parachuted to Tahiti
Where he ratified a treaty
For manganese and chives;
Then, disguised as Mr. Eden,
He was smuggled into Sweden
And adroitly played the lead in
Sabotage and *Private Lives*.
After lecturing the natives of Uganda
As propaganda
He met—while having tea with Marshal Tito—
A female spy who worked for Hirohito
And in his role
Of Britain's best ambassador
He made a shocking pass at her,
And Noël
Succeeded even with de Gaulle.

In a dressing-gown quite exquisitely flowered,
Mr. Coward
At the conferences which he daily sat on
Advised both Eisenhower and Mountbatten
On the private habits of the lower decks.
After turning up at G.H.Q. in Kandy
Disguised as Ghandi,

And retrieving missing papers from a taxi
Where they'd stupidly been left by Halifax, he
Gave a lecture to the R.A.F. on sex.
He escaped from Casablanca
On a rather sordid tanker
Which eventually dropped anchor
In the Duodecanese;
He created quite a flutter
By his comments on Calcutta,
Where he found the boredom utter
And had prickly heat and fleas.
He recovered stolen plans of Messrs. Vickers
From someone's knickers;
As an agent he was certainly no novice
But he found that working for the Foreign Office
Was quite a bore:
With Eden, life was Heaven there;
But on finding Ernest Bevin there
He swore
That he would spy no more.

One of the briefest and best revue lyrics in recent years was
the one—again not by me, I wish I had thought of it—
where a nun and a monk appeared side-by-side on the stage
and sang:

> If you were the only girl in the world
> And I were the only boy,
> Nothing—

At which point came the black-out.[1] It is like the other rather
sad one where the tenor starts singing 'Take Thou This Rose'
and the soprano takes it and walks off-stage.[2]

1. Acknowledgment to Peter Myers who thought of it.
2. Acknowledgment to whoever thought of it; it seems to have just
arrived in rehearsal.

9

I HAVE WORKED for the B.B.C., either on the staff or as a contributor or performer, for over forty years. They are a good firm to work for. At the time of writing they are in trouble; because of what some people consider a sinister document called *Broadcasting in the Seventies* the correspondence columns of *The Times* are bursting at the seams with indignant letters of protest from B.B.C. producers, University dons, former B.B.C. governors, M.P.s, clergymen and humble but het-up housewives. Lesser topics like Vietnam, pollution and test-tube babies have been edged out of the Printing House Square mailbag; even the annual letter from the gentleman who, for some strange reason, compiles a list of boys' and girls' Christian names in order of popularity was squeezed down to the foot of the page. (John and Mary, it may astound you, are still high up at the top of the pops.) No doubt by the time these lines appear, if they ever do, the B.B.C. brouhaha will have sorted itself out; I hope so. The Corporation's troubles stem from three main factors: money, ratings and Lord Hill. Mr. Wilson, at a time when he considered—perhaps with some justification—that the B.B.C. was biased against the Labour Party and particularly against himself, obviously thought "Right: I'll show them" and switched Lord Hill from I.T.V. to be Chairman of the B.B.C.'s Board of Governors. It was, as a senior member of the B.B.C. said at the time, like putting Rommel in command of our desert forces. The few Chairmen—or, come to that, Director-Generals—the Corporation has had in its lifetime have been fairly aloof characters, remote from the rank and file who actually plan or put out the programmes. They have influenced the general tone and character of the Corporation's output, and have played no small part in making it far and away the finest broadcasting service in the world. Which it is, even now; infinitely superior to American radio and television, far above the standards of any of the Continental networks. Reith was, of course, the first and greatest D.-G. He saw, even over forty years ago and long before television became a practical proposition, the influence the Corporation could exert either for good or ill; until now he has been one of the few to steer clear of *The Times* correspondence columns and the general hubbub, but he must be a very concerned man at the way things have gone and are going. He was a man of immense integrity, with a strength of personality to match that integrity; on the morning after that unfortunate but understandable "the Fleet's lit up" broadcast, I watched him arrive at Broadcasting House. The Press were there in droves outside the main entrance, baying like famished wolves for a statement. Reith simply got out of his car, crossed the pavement, cleft (if that is in fact the past tense of the verb to cleave) a path through them, and went into B.H. and up in the lift to his office without saying a word or looking to left or right. The Press stood aside and made way for him; you have to be a big man, not just in terms of feet and inches, for the British Press to do that when they are after a story.

Reith and his successors and their different Boards of Governors had left the creative people more or less alone and allowed them to get on with their job; unless some really serious gaffe was committed or something put out which cut directly across the laid-down policy of doing things which wouldn't offend too many people too often and at the same time doing them as well as possible, the D.-G. stayed put in his office, informed the Board of Governors at regular intervals how ably the Corporation was being governed, advised the Postmaster-General how to answer any awkward questions, entertained high-powered visitors to lunch, and rarely if ever was seen near a studio, let alone the canteen. Lord Hill is not the sort of person to stay put in his office and wait to be told what is going on; for one thing, he has been a professional broadcaster himself, specialising during his spell as the Radio Doctor in such delicate matters as our bladders, bronchial tubes and bowels; on his appointment there was an uneasy suspicion that the new boy might want to interfere a bit, might even turn up in a studio during rehearsal and say he didn't like the way things were being done. The suspicion proved not entirely unfounded. But the real cause of the present malaise is finance and, very much linked up with it, the rat-race after ratings. The Corporation is in money trouble and, because of the arrival of competition from the commercial channels and its decision to fight the opposition tooth and nail irrespective of standards or quality, it is likely to get deeper and deeper in the red. The thoroughly evil thing behind all this—as Milton Shulman keeps succinctly hammering home in the *Evening Standard*—is something that is totally unimportant to the listener or the viewer: ratings. Ratings are important, or can be made to appear important, to the advertisers and the public relations boys; they may on occasions boost an actor's or a writer's ego when they read that their shows have got in the top twenty or have notched up an alleged audience of 4,760,000 in the North-East. They couldn't matter less to the people who matter: the people who have seen or heard the show. All that matters to them is whether the show has been good, indifferent or bloody awful. In any case, in my view ratings—like public opinion polls—are highly suspect. I have never had any really solid faith in them since, many years ago, I was scheduled to produce a forty-five minute programme for the B.B.C. in Scotland. At the very last minute the leading lady was stricken by the palsy; the programme was cancelled and instead they played three-quarters-of-an-hour of gramophone records. The programme which never went out got what is known as an Audience Appreciation Figure of 57.4, or some such ridiculous amount. I was even congratulated by my boss on how greatly the programme had been appreciated. (It has just occurred to me, after all these years, that perhaps they were very good records.) But even more so today both channels—B.B.C. and commercial—look on the ratings as the be-all and end-all; I hear otherwise quite intelligent people in the B.B.C. Club at Television Centre purring with delight over the fact that their latest production has attracted over eleven million viewers. It doesn't seem to matter that, even if the figure is accurate, it is just possible that a certain percentage of the eleven million positively loathed the programme; it is quantity, not quality, that counts. The B.B.C.'s method of concocting these figures is the more reliable; the other side's technique is to attach a sort of meter to a relatively small number of sets; if the set is switched on, the meter registers this fact, a needle ticks away somewhere else, and the owner of the set and his family are computerised as being riveted to a certain programme and, what is more dishonest, enjoying it. I don't think I am really unique, but there are many occasions in my house when the telly is on and I am not taking a blind bit of notice of it; I have got so bored with a programme that I can't even be bothered to get up and switch the wretched thing off; I am either at the evening papers or a novel or have left the room to spend a penny or brew a cup of tea. But if I were one of the commercial television's faithful band of figure-riggers, the meter is still registering, the needle is still ticking away, and I am clocked in as being glued to whatever rubbish is on the box and revelling in it.

One of the sad things about the B.B.C.'s decision to become a slave to the ratings and fight its competitors on their own terms is that it gives the viewers not a choice but in many cases a carbon copy. If a 1942 Doris Day movie is on at eight o'clock on commercial, the Corporation in its desperation to cling to an audience puts on a 1941 Betty Grable at the same time. If the B.B.C. outside broadcasts unit put out a repeat of some big boxing match, the commercial boys do their damnedest to cap it with a repeat of a big football game. When David Attenborough was at its head, B.B.C.2 seemed to be the one channel in the world which didn't care a hoot about ratings; if they felt like devoting the entire evening to opera or ballet or tennis or whatever, they did so; and the hell with how many people watched, didn't watch, switched off, were bored stiff or enchanted. As a result, the channel produced some of the best things television has ever done; there are sorry signs that even B.B.C.2 is beginning to be rating-bound.

Part of the battle has, unfortunately, political implications. Even though their kitty was and is in a sad state, the B.B.C. elected to take on local radio in addition to their other commitments; they knew that, when or if the Conservatives were returned to power, that party was more or less committed to local radio being given to commercial interests. In a panic, if only because Mr. Wilson seemed at the time to be almost pleading for a change in government, they rushed the thing through with neither the finance nor the personnel available to do the job properly. They started with eight stations and at the time of writing are setting up some forty more, incidentally completely ravaging the accepted concept of regional broadcasting. The argument—a perfectly logical one—was that if a network of local radio stations was established before a change of government and was even only moderately successful, it would be very difficult indeed to undo the whole scheme and have the stations handed over to the commercial boys. I am a member of the advisory council for Radio Brighton; we meet monthly and proffer our advice (it is not always taken, but then perhaps it is not always good advice); the local station manager and his ridiculously small staff seem to me to accomplish miracles; but at the back of every problem which they and we face is one thing: money, or the lack of it. I have the feeling that if, say, Marks and Spencers or Sainsburys weighed in with a thousand or so a week in return for a thirty-second plug for their St. Michael briefs or their Israeli strawberries selling in February at four-and-six a punnet, local radio might be better. But don't say I said so.

Despite its present problems, the B.B.C. remains a remarkable institution, efficient and straight to work for, on its television side bursting with talent, on its sound radio side perhaps suffering somewhat from long-rooted dead wood. The really swinging centre of show business in London— the place where you star-gaze—is no longer a restaurant off Shaftesbury Avenue or a pub in St. Martin's Lane; it is one of the restaurants in Television Centre when the casts of perhaps six or more different productions are having their lunch break, or the club on the fourth floor at around six thirty in the evening when the last rehearsals are over and the same casts are having a drink—"No thanks, dear boy, not another: got to do the show at eight, and make-up want me at seven thirty." I find it intriguing to try to guess who is up to what when I share a table in the restaurant with two elderly character actresses in full Edwardian finery, a well-known face that I can't put a name to but whose owner is dressed as a policeman, and a sizzling dish in either the miniest of minis or the maxiest of maxis whom I am certain I have seen many times before but can't think whether it was in 'The Forsyte Saga' or 'Portrait of a Lady'. Apart from his name, the copper is easy to place; almost inevitably he is in 'Softly, Softly'; the two Edwardian ladies remain mysteries even when they leave the table and go, gracefully holding up their full-length skirts and adjusting their feather boas, to pay their bills at the cash-desk for their Welsh rarebit, apple crumble and coffee; the dish more often than not turns out to be some producer's secretary who has never acted in her life except on the phone. The unfair, but I suppose inevitable, thing is that it is the television side of the B.B.C.'s output which takes on this aura of glamour and excitement and gets most, if not all, of the headlines. Along at the end of the Strand—in Bush House—there is another empire churning out what is without doubt the most important and certainly the least publicised part of the output; sending out programmes in the B.B.C.'s External Services at all hours of the day and night and in pretty well every language from Arabic to Zulu. To be strictly accurate, in forty languages and for a total of one hundred hours of programme time every day. Again sorely pinched for money, this sector of the B.B.C. gets not a penny piece out of the licence fee. It is financed by the Treasury, and you know what Treasuries are. If the present or any future government ever digs into its coffers and gives the Corporation more cash, this is where a sizable proportion of the cash should go, not to provide even more lavish sets for the Rolf Harris show or even higher fees for me. I take that last remark back, the Glass Menagerie might be upset. But listeners in Budapest or Berlin or Bratislava or wherever trouble is brewing or has brewed still say (perhaps still whisper) as they did during World War II, "It must be true, I heard it on the B.B.C." Krushchev once banged his shoe with an almighty thud on the table at a United Nations session, and on getting back to the Kremlin repeated the performance to show the comrades just how emphatic he had been. At the encore, his shoe-lace broke and he had to go home without one. He was greeted by Mrs. Krushchev with a pair of shoe-laces in her hand. When Krushchev said, "How did you know?", that rather cosy-looking lady said simply, "I heard it on the B.B.C."

The old girl may have her troubles; lack of finance, threats of strikes and rebellions, letters to *The Times*, having the change at her time of life, and all the rest of it. What matters is that the old girl is still trusted. Few of the bright new boys in the Corporation would even think of it, let alone admit it, but, despite what sometimes seems to be deliberate attempts to throttle it, the influence of Reith is still there. If the foundations are properly laid, the building wears well; even if squatters get inside it or morons write graffiti on its lavatory walls.

For a writer, one of the many good things about working in television is that it works both ways. The companies can approach you, however cagily, and ask if by any chance you happen to have an idea which might just possibly be right for so-and-so; the writer can buttonhole someone who matters in the companies and—after the third or fourth gin—drop in the fact that he happens to have rather a good idea for so-and-so who, by the most remarkable coincidence, he happens to know is available and would not be averse to doing a television series. In 1968 Frank Muir, who was then in charge of the comedy side of the B.B.C.'s Light Entertainment division, rang me and asked if I had an idea for a Comedy Playhouse; these are shows which, if you are lucky and they are successful, more often than not spin off into series. Frank is someone who knows almost all that needs to be known about both writing comedy and acting in it; he has done a considerable amount of both. His departure from the B.B.C. to London Weekend was a sad loss to the B.B.C.; his exit from London Weekend when the bomb went up in that set-up was an equally sorry loss to them. I said yes, for once I had an idea. I had been flogging with no success at all a comedy about a duck; actually it was a mallard. The mallard had waddled from its natural habitat in St. James's Park—it was a female, and pregnant—across Horse Guards Parade, into the Foreign Office, and had settled down snugly in the out-tray of the Foreign Secretary's desk. She was sitting on a number of vitally important papers which called for immediate action, but because of the Island Race's noted softness for our feathered or four-footed friends it was agreed that it was out of the question to move her from the out-tray until she had hatched out. The mallard's normal period of incubation is around three weeks; the point of the piece, if any, was that because of the mallard—she was called Barbara, after Mrs. Castle—sitting there on all those tremendously important papers and nothing being done about them for three weeks, all the problems the Foreign Office had on their plate at the time automatically resolved themselves. The West End managements had turned the play down unanimously as being too far-fetched; as a matter of fact, some months after it was written, a duck—it so happens, a mallard—waddled from the lake in St. James's Park and established herself, not in an out-tray in the Foreign Office, but on a hot-plate in the kitchens of the House of Lords. The same thing happened; the kitchen staff refused to have it ejected until it had finished the job on hand and no doubt Their Lordships' menus suffered during the period of propagation. Frank Muir said, "It's a sort of modern fable, isn't it? ... I've got a slot for it in 'Comedy Playhouse' five weeks on Thursday." This was a show called 'The Minister's Mallard' starring Moira Lister and Robert Coote, out of which came a series called 'The Whitehall Worrier', out of which came three series called 'The Very Merry Widow', starring Moira on her own. That is the way these things work; not always, but sometimes.

In recent years I have thought it sensible to get away from the television studios for a few weeks and go into rep; check up if you still can put it across, still time the laughs correctly with a real audience who have actually paid to come in, still be heard at the back of the circle without the help of microphones tucked inside your shirt or up your crutch, and booms following you around like autograph-hunters. I have done the duck play—under the title *Top Priority*—in repertory at Northampton and Bromley; I drank more tea in the little green-room at Northampton Rep., and had more fun with the resident members of the company than I have ever drunk or had in my life. The same thing happened at Bromley; I think, when one added up the hotel bills and travelling expenses, I was severely out of pocket; my agents thought I had taken leave of my senses. But it was a kind of therapy, and well worth it.

'The Whitehall Worrier' and 'The Very Merry Widow' reunited me with Moira Lister, not that we had ever stayed any great distance apart since *The Gazebo* days. She is a remarkable person; she is a hundred per cent professional; she arrives at rehearsal on the dot (in the Rolls, naturally, but that doesn't matter, the thing is that she would be there on the dot if she had to come on a bike); she has done her homework; she works like the hardest working of those idiotic Trojans; she is fun and rightly intolerant only of other people's inefficiency or slackness. There are very few glamorous ladies around today who can be funny and stay glamorous. Lucille Ball over on the other side; Moira on this; after that you have to think. She is an incredible mixture of the Belgravia-based Vicomtesse with a villa in Cap d'Ail and the down-to-brass-tacks actress who, when called on to be in some God-forsaken location at some unearthly hour in the morning to film a difficult scene in the pouring rain, does it —and what is more is ready to go on doing it all day until it is right. Behind the glamour, she is a tough, efficient, athletic South African with unbelievable energy; when we had a holiday together at Eze-sur-mer and swam out to the raft the Widow was aboard it considerably ahead of me with her expert crawl making my plodding breast-stroke look very soppy indeed. As I said earlier, during the run of *The Gazebo* we rarely, if ever, stopped laughing; the same thing happened during those three years on television. But there is something much more important than just being a lovely lady who likes laughing and making other people laugh. In the foreword I wrote to her own book *The Very Merry Moira*—also published by this admirable firm of Hodder and Stoughton, who obviously select their authors with care and perspicacity—I said she was great to work with. It wasn't I who originally said it, though I have always thought it; it was a tough, out-size scene-shifter standing in the wings one night watching her do a 'Very Merry Widow' show. He nudged me as he said it (I get nudged by all sorts of people) and he obviously meant it. When the boys on the studio floor do that it means more than a rave notice from Peter Black or Maurice Wiggin or Philip Purser, grateful though one always is to these gentle-men and the rest of their ilk when they write something nice about you.

In the last two or three years, as well as 'The Whitehall Worrier' and 'The Very Merry Widow', I have done two series based on Sir Alan Herbert's 'Misleading Cases' with Alastair Sim and Roy Dotrice, two series of 'Before the Fringe', and a number of single productions including two up-dated versions of Gilbert and Sullivan: *The Mikado* and *Iolanthe*. It has been non-stop television; I have had one holi-day in the three years. Not that I am complaining; well, I complain about the holiday. I had a free fortnight in 1969 and went to Biot, which is—or was before they began build-ing hideous blocks of flats all round it—a delightful little village just outside Antibes. The first course of the first meal on my first night in the hotel was fruits de mer gratinée; it was so gratinée that it was difficult to diagnose what fruits had come out of which mer. Halfway through the dish I had the feeling that all was not well; but, as one usually does on these occasions, I plodded on. I spent the next three days and nights either on the loo or kneeling in front of it in a position of prayer; I have never felt so ill in my life. When on the morning of the fourth day a doctor was summoned and said he would like me to go into the British Hospital in Nice for a check-up, I panicked, doped myself to the eyeballs, grabbed a cancelled seat on the first plane from Nice, and flew home. Marty Feldman and his wife were waiting at the bar in the airport to catch the same plane; when he asked me what I would have and I said a small Perrier water his eyes swivelled even more than usual.

The modernised Gilbert and Sullivans were preceded with every possible manifestation of horror; the Savoyards began grouping for the attack; how dare I, of all people, tamper with Holy Writ. On the night we did *Titipu*—the tampered version of *The Mikado* with Cyril Ritchard superb as the Mikado, Hattie Jacques brilliant as Katisha, and Harry Worth being not only very funny as Ko-Ko but amazing me by being the first person who has ever made the 'Tit-Willow' song really moving—I was laid on to appear on 'Late Night Line-Up' to face an infuriated mob of G. and S. diehards after my scalp. It was a terrible flop; even the life members of the Gilbert and Sullivan Society whom they tried to get in to scalp me all said they'd rather enjoyed it. Amateur Operatic Societies still write in to ask if they can do the tampered version instead of the original. Again it was a fascinating exercise in lyric-writing; all I really did was what Gilbert, I am sure, would have done if he had been writing the show today; he wrote lyrics which were crammed with topical allusions; he was enough of a professional not to want them to sound out-of-date. The Lord Chancellor's famous nightmare song in *Iolanthe* is full of lines which must have been big laughs at the time it was written, but which are more or less meaningless today; references to bathing-machines and banburys, and phrases like "ties play the dealer". What that means I have no idea. Supplied with the splendid original pattern of the lyric, it was a delight to be given the chance to try to make it right for the late sixties. In the revised version, the first two lines and the last five are Gilbert's, or almost Gilbert's; the rest, I am afraid, are mine. Once again, I don't know how I had the nerve . . .

When you're lying awake with a splitting headache
And all sleep is taboo'd by anxiety
And for hour after hour you are apt to turn sour
On all aspects of modern society,
You put all the blame on—don't mention the name—but
The leader of one certain Party
Who has reached his high rank saying "let me be frank"
But is clearly a smoothie or smarty.
Then—you're tossing and turning, your forehead now
    burning—
And changing again your position
You consider the deeds of the fellow who leads
Such a spineless, inept Opposition.
Then the bed seems to tilt and your eiderdown quilt
Disappears like a trick by magicians
And you're out in a sweat and you want to forget
All parties and all politicians;
So you think (rather late) you must now concentrate
On some rather more likable sector
But the one thing you find in your turbulent mind
Is the tax that you owe the Collector.
As you lie there in bed, you can see it—in red
That final demand that he sent you;
And your future looks blank, since the man from the Bank
Has remembered how much he has lent you.
You've a sore, hacking cough but at last you doze off
And get plunged in an absolute nightmare;
You're presented at Court in apparel so short
It's the kind that Godiva well might wear.
Then the Queen says "Goodbye, from my husband and I"
And she asks for your hand just to shake it;
But the whole thing's caput, since you give her your foot
And are left in the Throne Room, stark naked.
Then the scene quickly changes and someone arranges
You're to swim in a race 'cross the Channel

Wearing wellington boots and three Harris tweed suits
And thick underwear made of red flannel;
And you're halfway across, but it's all a dead loss
For before you can say "tantarara",
Of the sea there's no trace and it seems that the race
Has been switched to the distant Sahara.
Then the nightmare gets worse, and you're due to rehearse
In a play by some avant-garde wizards;
You don't know what you're at; the director's a bat
And the rest of the actors are lizards.
And there comes the first night and you're shaking with
    fright
But you get to the playhouse in Chester;
Which is probably wise, for you find with surprise
That the play's being put on in Leicester.
Since it's too far to hike, you then borrow a bike
But you find that the pedals are missing;
By the time you reach Stoke you have only one spoke
And all thoughts of the play you're dismissing;
So you stop for a meal at an inn which, you feel,
Will be pleasantly quiet and relaxing;
There is only one space and he's there, face to face—
The Collector who does all your taxing.
Still, you order foie gras and some nice caviare
And a bottle of excellent claret,
And get cold Irish stew and a sauce made of glue
And some wine that's home-made; maybe carrot.
You both shiver and sweat with the sheets wringing wet
Or at least very damp and your left leg has cramp
And your pillow, what's more, has now slipped to the floor
And the mattress has things more like spanners than springs
And the clock in the tower strikes thirteen on the hour;
Your pyjamas feel tight and the cramp's switched to right;
You've a thirst that's intense and a general sense
That you haven't been sleeping in clover;

215

But the torture has passed and it's daylight at last
And the night has been long—ditto, ditto, this song—
And thank goodness they're both of them over!...

It is, you will agree, quite a mouthful. Patrick Cargill, who played the Lord Chancellor and was, as always, very funny indeed, was certainly glad when it was over. What with saddling Cicely Courtneidge with 'Vitality' and Mr. Cargill with this little job, I think I must have a slightly sadistic lyrical streak. There was a splendid moment when in a lunch break in the last week of rehearsing *Iolanthe* I said to Patrick, "You know, if you get an encore for the nightmare song— which you're bound to do—I've written a completely different lyric about *another* nightmare." For a very few fraught seconds Mr. Cargill believed me. He has a very expressive face; it has never expressed more.

In the sort of business people like myself are in, there are bound to be ups and downs; I have had my full share of both. The only thing to do with the downs is not to let them get you down and to start working on something else as quickly as possible in the hope that the graph will take an upward trend. The greatest satisfaction to me is to be still at it; still able to wake up in the morning and say, "Well, we know what we've got to do today." I can think of nothing worse than to wake up with not an idea in one's head and no prospect of work; I could, I suppose, ask to be taken back into the family timber business, but I feel it is a little late in life to start all over again as a joiner. I am in my sixties; I don't feel it, though there are mornings when—gazing sombrely at myself in the shaving-mirror—I look even older than the one hundred and two I settled for with Margaret Leighton. But it is good to be still accepted, however prehistoric; not totally written off as a has-been; not, which is much worse, mooning around moaning about the good old days and how everything has changed for the worse. It hasn't. Not so long ago I was on the Cilla Black show; it gave me a kick to work with that very talented youngster and be treated, not as an old fossil to whom she had to be respectful, but simply as one of the gang with whom she could even crack gags about the Motown. When you slither or hobble into the sixties, some of the teen-agers assume that senility must have set in almost by right; I did a quiz programme not long ago about pop and when I said that, so far as I was concerned, Roy Orbison could do no wrong, my team-mates on the panel seemed taken aback. After the show one of them said to me, "I didn't think people like you *knew* about Roy Orbison."

It has been a lovely, full, happy life; I have few regrets about it—the main one being that I would have liked to have had a son—and I have a very great deal to be thankful for. I have known and worked with many wonderful people, not just the stars, but people like the kids in Northampton Rep., the stage hand in the television show who nudged me and said, "She's great to work with, isn't she, guv'nor?" or Midge, my lady what does, who charges up the stairs from the kitchen with my lunch and is heard muttering halfway up, "This time I really *will* have to go." What happens from now on, I wouldn't know; fortunately no-one does. Tomor-row morning the Glass Menagerie may ring up with news of some fabulous job; tomorrow afternoon the B.B.C. may be on the blower saying that the series we have been discussing has unfortunately but unavoidably been cancelled. The num-ber which was the finale of *Sweetest and Lowest* perhaps sums up the whole thing . . .

What next? . . .
How best to end the show?
What next? . . .
Nobody seems to know.
Should we be rather glamorous or amorous or what?

Conclude the thing satirically or lyrically, or not?
What next? . . .
Before the curtain falls—
What next? . . .
Before those curtain calls—
In dealing with the future we're uncertain;
The only thing that's certain
Is the curtain.

INDEX